W9-AOB-512

Epitaph

APOLOGY: Index numbering a Bit off Corrected in Later Printings.

EPITAPH

Extremism

(ANACHRONISM, ANARCHISM,
INFANTILISM, NIHILISM)

Or A

More Perfect Union

(BREACH OR BRIDGE
MESSAGE TO AMERICA)

NonViolence THE BETTER WAY

Dr. CAROLYN LaDELLE BENNETT

Copyright © 2022 by Dr. Carolyn LaDelle Bennett.

Library of Congress Control Number: 2022914397
ISBN: Hardcover   978-1-6698-2495-4
               Softcover   978-1-6698-2496-1
               eBook   978-1-6698-2497-8

All rights reserved. No part of this book may be reproduced or transmitted in any form or by any means, electronic or mechanical, including photocopying, recording, or by any information storage and retrieval system, without permission in writing from the copyright owner.

Any people depicted in stock imagery provided by Getty Images are models, and such images are being used for illustrative purposes only.
Certain stock imagery © Getty Images.

Print information available on the last page.

Rev. date: 08/10/2022

To order additional copies of this book, contact:
Xlibris
844-714-8691
www.Xlibris.com
Orders@Xlibris.com
828689

CONTENTS

A DEDICATION PLEDGE

I PLEDGE ALLEGIANCE
To the flag and to the Republic for which it stands
One Nation, *Indivisible*
Long live the *Union* of these States of America!

Squandered Legacy

The *betrayal* continues. It is a betrayal that does not end with violating the people of contemporary America. It is a betrayal that dishonors America's revolutionaries against tyranny, its founders and framers of a new government—a great legacy left for later generations to build upon. It is a betrayal of all those American men and women, down through the years, from the eighteenth through the twentieth centuries, who rose from and served in places like Braintree and Weymouth, Massachusetts; Philadelphia and Gettysburg, Pennsylvania; the Chesapeake; Hodgenville, Kentucky; Holly Springs and Ruleville, Mississippi; and Houston, Texas—honorable men and women who reinforced, defined, and redefined the founding principles, and worked to preserve and protect the Union.

America's Constitutional Convention in Philadelphia between May 25 and September 17, 1787, was one of the most important events in the history of the United States of America. Its crowning achievement was laying the foundation of a new frame of government. This act brought an end to the notion of "divine right of kings" and replaced the Articles of Confederation with a new Constitution *"in Order to form a more perfect Union, establish Justice, insure domestic Tranquility, provide for the common defense, promote the general Welfare, and secure the Blessings of Liberty to ourselves and our Posterity."*

The campaign for the new Constitution was led by revolutionaries and framers of that Constitution. Alexander Hamilton, James Madison, and John Jay wrote articles and essays interpreting the text of the proposed constitution and making the case for it. Their essays were written under the collective pseudonym "Publius" and published during the period of October 1787 and April 1788 (nos. 1–77) in New York newspapers the *Independent Journal*, the *New York Packet*, and the *Daily Advertiser*.

The collection of articles was known as *The Federalist* (much later *The Federalist Papers*). The proposed Constitution was ratified on June 21, 1788; and toward the end of July 1788, the process of organizing the new government began.

Publius has been defined as having the same root as *populous* and *publicus*, which means "the people" or "of the people."[1]

The founders' weaving of the Constitution and the Union and their warnings about factionalism and disunion are pertinent in the current context as it is deeply concerned about the breach inside contemporary America: the extremism, the rabid and violent nature of leadership, media and influential factions (setting the example for the rest of society), the continued breakdown of law and disestablishment of essential institutions meant to be of, by, and for the people; a destructive pandering, whimsical anything-goes anarchism and nihilism; a contradictory, schizophrenic anachronism uninformed by the past; a perilous regress enabled by incompetence, corruption, and willful ignorance that leaves America in a chronic state of unpreparedness and ill health. The consequences are dire, far reaching into US foreign affairs, and dangerously ricocheting.

Weakness and divisions inside invite dangers from outside, John Jay wrote in *Federalist* No. 5; and nothing provides more security than union, strength within, and good government.

In this moment of compounding crises and destructive tendencies among incestuously entrenched public officials and their partners and reactionary tribes, it is essential to pause and reconsider the voices of

---

[1] https://en.wikipedia.org/wiki/Publius_(praenomen)

America's founders and framers of government. *The Federalist Papers'* stress of Union and fear of opposition to Union was as important now as it was in Hamilton's time. It may seem "superfluous to offer arguments to prove the utility of the Union," Hamilton wrote in *Federalist* No. 1. Surely the notion is "deeply engraved on the hearts of the great body of the people in every State." Yet there were whispers of opposition to the new Constitution.

Consider today's entrenched bought and bossed Congress on Capitol Hill and the incestuous revolving door of lobbyists and academics, weapons, profiteering nonprofit industrial complexes.

The framers of the Constitution in eighteenth-century America warned of a kleptocratic, or self-interested, class of men set on resisting all changes that may hazard a diminution of their power, emolument, and hold on state establishments; the perverted ambition of another class of men, who will either hope to aggrandize themselves before the public, or flatter themselves with prospects of elevation in breakaway confederacies from the Union under one government.

Today's anti-Union factions can be found not only among state leaders and political partisans but also in every imaginable segment of society; and careless of the nation's founding, they are continually multiplying. To be fair, some anti-Unionists, the framers observed, may be suffering from errors of judgment driven by preconceived jealousies and fears. Even wise and good people may find themselves "on the wrong side, as well as on the right side" of questions critical to the well-being of a whole society. "Ambition, avarice, personal animosity, party opposition, and many other motives not more laudable than these are apt to operate … upon those who support, as those who oppose, the right side of a question."

Now as then, adherents to political parties and other sectarian entities, set on enabling themselves are notorious for instigating division to obtain and retain their power. By the loudness of their declamations and the bitterness of their invectives, they "hope to demonstrate the justness of their opinions, and to increase the number of their converts."

In the quest for power and retention of power, government is demonized, and its efficiency deliberately impaired. In the current era, one of the leading anti-government icons (with a careless cult following of more than forty years) was the B-movie actor Ronald Reagan, who was allowed to lead the state of California (now in utter disrepair) and was elevated to Washington (from which all of America's crumbling originates).

Those who "have overturned the liberties of republics" often launched their careers "by paying obsequious court to the people, commencing demagogues (using popular prejudices, false claims, offering promises to gain power); and ending (their careers as) tyrants."

The framers warned of the failure to understand that a "noble enthusiasm" for liberty may camouflage "a spirit of narrow and illiberal distrust," and that strong government is essential for the preservation of liberty.

A dangerous ambition more often lurks behind the specious mask of zeal for the rights of the people than under the forbidden appearance of zeal for the firmness and efficiency of government.

The framers of a new form of government declared the indispensability, the imperative of the Union without which "the safety and welfare of the parts," *the nation itself,* are threatened.

The prosperity of the people of America depends on "their continuing firmly united," John Jay said in *Federalist* No. 2 as he made the case for the Union. The first and succeeding congresses — congresses composed of "wise and experienced" people of "sound judgment" and "integrity" worthy of the trust of the people—and the late convention joined with the people in believing that America's prosperity depends on its Union and that "to preserve and perpetuate the Union" was the aim of those who formed the original convention in Philadelphia.

In the American Revolutionary era, the First and Second Continental Congresses were formed and met in 1774 and 1775–1781, respectively. On July 2, 1776, the Congress resolved unanimously that the thirteen "United Colonies" were and by right ought to be "free and independent states." On July 4, 1776, the Congress approved this Declaration of Independence and prepared the Articles of Confederation. In March 1781, after approval by the states, the Articles of Confederation became America's first Constitution, which remained in effect until 1789. Its successor was the Constitution of the United States, written during the Constitutional Convention in Philadelphia, Pennsylvania, May 14 through September 17, 1787.

"I sincerely wish," Jay concluded,

> that it may be as clearly foreseen by every good citizen, that whenever the dissolution of the **Union** arrives, America will have reason to exclaim, in the words of the poet: 'FAREWELL— A LONG FAREWELL TO ALL MY GREATNESS.'"

John Jay was born in British America's New York City (December 12, 1745). He was among the founders of the United States of America, a leading Federalist, an abolitionist, and statesman, diplomat, negotiator, lawyer, and public official. He died in Bedford, New York, on May 17, 1829. His public service included the following:

- Delegate from New York to the Second Continental Congress (May 10, 1775 – May 22, 1776; December 7, 1778 – September 28, 1779)
- Sixth President of the Continental Congress (December 10, 1778–September 28, 1779)

- United States Minister to Spain (Appointed by the Second Continental Congress, September 27, 1779–May 20, 1782)
- United States Secretary of Foreign Affairs (appointed by the Congress of the Confederation, December 21, 1784–March 3, 1789; under President Washington, July 27, 1789–September 15, 1789)
- Acting United States Secretary of State (September 15, 1789–March 22, 1790)
- Second governor of New York (July 1, 1795–June 30, 1801)
- First Chief Justice of the United States (October 19, 1789–June 29, 1795)

Born in the Caribbean (circa January 11, 1755 or 1757), Alexander Hamilton became one of the founders of the United States of America and a leading supporter and interpreter of the Constitution of the United States. He is credited with founding the nation's financial system, the United States Coast Guard, and the *New York Post* newspaper. He died of a gunshot wound in New York City, New York, on July 12, 1804. His public service included the following:

- Delegate from New York to the Congress of the Confederation (November 4, 1782–June 21, 1783; November 3, 1788–March 2, 1789)
- Senior Officer of the United States Army (under President John Adams: December 14, 1799–June 15, 1800)
- First United States Secretary of the Treasury (under President Washington: September 11, 1789–January 31, 1795)

Some seventy years after Hamilton and Jay's *Federalist* and the framing of the Constitution of the United States, and in another moment of great strife, came another devout supporter of the Union, a son of the Heartland—Abraham Lincoln. On the road to the presidency, Lincoln was heard to say, "If we could know where we are and to what place we appear to be tending, we could better judge what to do and how to do it. ... I do not expect the Union to be dissolved—I do not expect the house to fall. ... I do expect it will cease to be divided: It will become all one thing or all the other...." (1858 separate occasions)

At Gettysburg, President Lincoln said, "It is ... for us to be dedicated to the great task remaining before us... that we here highly resolve ... that this nation... shall have a new birth of freedom; and that government of the people, by the people, for the people shall not perish from the earth" ("Gettysburg Address," delivered November 19, 1863).

"With malice toward none," Lincoln declared, on entering his second term as America's sixteenth president, "with charity for all; with firmness in the right... as (we are given) to see the right—let us strive on ...

> To finish the work we are in
>
> To bind up the nation's wounds
>
> To care for (those) who shall have borne the battle; and for (their relations)
>
> To do all which may achieve and cherish a just and a lasting peace among ourselves—*and with all nations.* (Minor edits, emphasis added)

Abraham Lincoln was America's sixteenth president. He was known as Honest Abe, the Rail-Splitter, the Great Emancipator. Lincoln was a great orator and debater, a practicing lawyer and statesman, a self-taught philosopher, a member of the Illinois Militia Officer (1832); a member of the Illinois House of Representatives (Sangamon County, December 1, 1834–December 4, 1842), and a member of the US House of Representatives (Seventh District, Illinois, March 4, 1847–March 3, 1849) before assuming the duties of America's president (March 4, 1861–April 15, 1865).

He was born in Hodgenville, Kentucky, on February 12, 1809, the son of Thomas Lincoln and Nancy Hanks (his family moved to

Illinois when he was twenty-one); husband of Mary Todd; father of Robert, Edward, Willie, and Tad Lincoln. Like Alexander Hamilton (in different circumstances at age forty-eight) sixty-one years earlier, Abraham Lincoln's life was taken at age fifty-six, on April 15, 1865, by a gunman's bullet.

INTRODUCTION

Extremism

Americans do not think of themselves as extremists, or of their actions as manifestations of extremism. To them, it is always the *other* person, place, or thing that is extremist—the other guy, the other nation, the other group that is the extremist. It becomes a mantra, often a slanderous mantra spread far and wide.

Extremism means "off the charts" in excessiveness, unreasonableness: fanatical, rabid, unconscionable, violent, wild. In contemporary America, "left" and "right" are so far off that they bond in extremism: in their fanaticism and their out-of-control aggression in matters domestic and transnational, at home and abroad.

From public officials to the leadership class and their revolving door (incestuous) cohorts from Stanford and Berkeley to Harvard and Yale, DuPont Circle and K Street; Bethesda, Maryland, and Pentagon City, Northern Virginia. From the Bush and Clinton clan to the "Samanthas" and "Victorias," the "Antonys" and "Austins," down the line to the professional "racialists," lecturers, indoctrinators, and their prey. Americans *are* extremists, and their extremism is like a disease spread throughout the population.

A common manifestation is *infantilism* seen in their mentally regressive tendencies:

- To *blame* others for acts they have committed
- To *bully* (as if on a playground but far more treacherous than ever found on a schoolyard)

- To *bribe* or beat others into submission, or complicity in the cover-up of their misdeeds

And armed with lethal weapons and/or acute arrogance, deliberate ignorance, and unspeakable cowardice, they *refuse* to reflect on and own up to their wrongs. They refuse to shoulder the responsibility for themselves. Refuse to right the wrongs, mend, and move forward.

American extremism is foisted upon the world every day all day through major media and an array of public figures' delusional declaration of (a kind of pledge of allegiance to) *exceptionalism* which, as its name implies, is perfection needless of correction. The maker of laws is *bound by none.*

Americans' extremism can be seen in the following:

- *Anachronism*: Backwardness, reversion to caveman aggression, rabid individualism, and unilateralism that claims *convenient* "allies" and *convenient* "enemies"
- *Anarchism*: In which anything goes—lawlessness, chaos, corruption legalized, traditions, social standards, essential societal principles, rules banished
- *Nihilism*: Tendency to destroy self and others, self-annihilation, and, in squandering America's founding legacy, destruction of the United States of America

Americans' extremism, in many ways mentally depraved and incestuous in nature, has succeeded in hollowing out the heart of America, leaving the country decrepit and dying.

What will be the course forward? Will there *be* a course forward?

The *liberals* and *neoliberals* and the "progressives" and "conservatives" (we are what we do, not what we say) are *of a kind* — self-serving, warmongering dividers and manipulators ripping up the founding legacy (often trivializing or debasing it), building nothing, and leaving a nation broken, a people wanting and unprepared for the future.

The battling wastrels in Congress and the color-coded, hyphenated individuals, groups and geographical regions, the ghettoed and gated (all the same) social and economic castes are, by their nature, incapable of moving America forward.

A nation dying of self-inflicted mental and moral wounds turns rabid—*extremist*. Leadership crippled by corruption, moral impairment, physical and mental decay is unable to do anything except the same old thing—commit violence by act or order and blame the acts, orders, and consequences on others.

Crippled leadership cripples and a nation. Thus America is enfeebled and on its death bed. The old-timers, the kleptocrats and gerontocrats, have a stranglehold on power and progress. And they continue to receive blind support from ordinary Americans (a citizenry suffering lost hope, careless of citizenry duty) because the leadership cabal has so corrupted and commandeered institutions and systems of government, silenced or censored truth so much so that *we the People of these United States* are denied any actual choice.

Words written and performed by 1970s band War and recorded in 2016 by singer, songwriter, pianist Kandace Springs seem to echo in the mind, though perhaps for different reasons: "The world is a ghetto."

Instead of lifting people up and ending the harm, United States leadership has conspired to turn the world into battling ghettos (or gates), communities that are no longer neighborly. From the United Nations down to local town neighborhoods, all that is left are mantras: "thoughts and prayers" and days of remembrance for the dead. Human rights in a state of unchecked and uncorrected abuse all over the world become Human Rights Day. Human trafficking all over the world becomes Human Trafficking Day. Armistice becomes a celebration of unending war.

There are days commemorating the dead, dying, and disabled; days of infirmity, poverty, and sickness of various kinds; days commemorating water and food shortages, unclean air and water and food waste, days of homelessness and illiteracy. Death and dying and disease and crime are commemorated as people holding the reins of power shamelessly perpetrate and exacerbate these ills. By design and deliberate acts, they never end them: never solve problems or cure disease or end suffering—*only the opposite.* With US officials at the helm, there is never actual *peace (nonviolence), only addiction; never a true ending of war, never actual cures of disease, never ending of want for the absolute basics such as shelter, decent living-wage work, nutritious food and clean water.*

Curable and preventable illnesses and basic research and development in and for nations and the world (including the United States) languish. Millions of people suffer while American money (and debt) supports the lifestyles of profiteers attached to religious entities like catholic charities and other profiteering nonprofit, non-governmental, think tank contractors and an array of contracting killers and anarchists spread across the world.

By the hand of US leadership, United Nations days commemorate the death of the United Nations itself; death of its original intentions and purposes for real peace as nonviolence. Replacing the United Nations' founding purposes are armed and violent, disease-spreading, human rights and sexual-abusing "peacekeepers." The New York City–headquartered United Nations is a bloated US tool (193 nations and layers upon layers of agencies and agents) complemented by the bloated Brussels-headquartered US tool of unspeakable violence—the North Atlantic Treaty Organization (NATO).

These are some of the unchecked and unchastened extremes in an anachronistic leadership cabal ensconced in and around Washington, contributing to the death of *one nation indivisible* (and of many other nations) by self-made wounds.

The choice is *more extremism* or a *more perfect Union.*

Will Americans continue their extremism? Or will they come together, mend their brokenness, and, with mutual respect for one another's gifts and abilities, work to form and further a more perfect Union—a living, breathing reality that brings substantive benefit and advancement, true goodness, peace, and uplift not only to America and Americans but also to the whole world and its people.

This effort seeks to illustrate Americans' extremism and its consequential state of unpreparedness, decline, and death. I use the term "Americans" instead of "America" deliberately because it is people (leaders, major media reporters, editors, analysts, broadcasters and sundry personalities, politicians, public officials and their cohorts and paymasters, sycophants, and members of the general public) who, in one way or another, are orchestrating the death of the nation.

In its first three chapters, the book lays out the nature of extremism and uses headlines, text, and information sources far from the inner circles of Washington, Los Angeles, New England, and New York City to show concrete evidence of Americans' dangerous and self-annihilating extremism. The final chapter brings text intended as solutions, corrections, sage advice to America's leaders (America needs new breeds of leaders)—if they are to summon the courage to end the incestuous corruption, join US state leaders in fixing the brokenness, bring America into the present, and, with other nations and peoples, move forward into a better future.

Sources and further information notes are placed centrally, appended to each chapter as part 2 to provide further evidence that has been documented or suggested in readings that Americans may not access but which have bearing on the chapter's focused content. Further, I want the reader to contrast or sense significant differences between what is produced, aired, written, reported, entered in official press releases or pronouncements, messaged through entertainment and other mass media originating in the United States; with what is written, aired, or otherwise reflected in news, information, and other official sources beyond the Washington Beltway and beyond the United States, more generally.

It is important to read foreign sources for several reasons. First, while US officials have touted press freedom, they have, at the same time, used conglomerate technology firms and the powers of the US government to censor, ban outright, and disparage press organizations such those originating from the Islamic Republic of Iran, the People's Republic of China, and the Russian Federation as "enemies" and "foreign agents." Second, officials in power and their cohorts have attacked individuals inside and outside the United States who practice or attempt to practice independent journalism. At the same time, they have used the American press as surveillance agents at home and abroad; and generally, as press release readers and copiers, stenographers, parrots of partisan, narrow-minded, divisive ideological positions.

Third, and perhaps most important, is the fact that a deliberately blinded and deafened citizenry, a citizenry that is deliberately ignorant cannot be a *responsible* citizenry.

The people of the United States, as preservers of their Union, must commit also to the freedom of other nations to have their brand of *union*.

The world is fast moving, immediate, and multifaceted; and Americans cannot afford to dig themselves into caves or ghettoes (no matter how these terms are defined). Americans must avail themselves of the clearest, cleanest, and most complete view of the world, the most unbiased and honest view of the world's nations and peoples. They must demand of themselves also the clearest possible documentation of the actions of their nation's leaders and the consequences of these actions.

Extremism: Anachronism, Gerontocracy

T HE SEAT OF United States federal governance, Washington District of Columbia, sets the example for the rest of the country and shines its light on the world in being dominated by moribund, static, somnambulant old men and women partnering with (and on the payroll of) an array of revolving-door egoists—unabashed, careless incompetents with a clamp on the self-serving status quo that is seriously weakening the United States as it attempts as well to the drag the whole world into antiquity.

Anachronism means "backwardness," and it is manifested in the US gerontocracy and demonstrable decay and ruin.

We hold these truths to be self-evident, the American Revolutionaries declared. *All* are created equal.

> They are endowed by their Creator with certain unalienable [inalienable] Rights. Among these rights are Life, Liberty and [a chance]. ...
>
> Whenever any Form of Government becomes destructive of these ends, it is the Right of the People to alter or abolish it; and to institute new Government, laying its foundation on such principles and organizing its powers in such form, as to them shall seem most likely to [produce, provide, ensure] their Safety and

Happiness." (Excerpt, minor edit in phrasing and word usage)

Ordinary Americans must hear and heed America's founding revolutionaries.

The contemporary crop of US officials (in and around Washington and the individual states), together with their partners, fail miserably to measure up to or meet any objective standards of fitness in terms of their mental, moral, intellectual, or psychological character, or their demonstrated diligence and care for this Union—the nation and its people. Officials' boasts of *patriotism* are mere bluster, tattered flags circling dealerships, pledging allegiance to commerce.

Gerontocrats
An Anachronistic Body of Destroyers

While ripping apart the fabric of this nation, American leaders, various public figures, and individuals associated with one or another form of media would have impressionable people believe that America is "better than all the rest."

This is a childish notion and a manipulative gesture. The repeated, mind-manipulating "We are better than all the rest" (*exceptionalism*) mantra is an illustration of US leaders' insidious drive to bring down the country. The psychological suggestion turns Americans' attention from the careless weakening of their country. "We are better than all the rest" is a delusional rally-round-a-tattered-flag (constant "enemy," constant aggression) cover-up of US leaders' irresponsibility; their ineptitude; their crisis-building failure to ensure the basic preparedness (health, education welfare) of the nation and its people.

The better-than-all-the-rest delusion (evident in some form across tribal identities, trappings, and leanings) renders the nation incapable of self-reflection and correction. It is a major driver in America's *backwardness*—a violence-prone, blood-soaked *anachronism* played out in the streets and neighborhoods of America, in the US Congress, and in the quality and character of US actions relating to other nations. America's citizens can no longer depend on, assume, or take for granted that the men and women who presume to lead, who contend for leadership positions, or who represent America are good and wise, people of sound judgment and integrity, people capable of common decency and respect for self and others.

In the midst of a pandemic that could not be covered up, Julius Krein wrote of America's diseased establishment.

> The specific problems of America's scientific gerontocracy... are best epitomized by the seventy-nine-year-old Dr. Anthony Fauci, who has bizarrely emerged as a media hero.

The government of former president Donald Trump deserves criticism "for its astonishing incompetence," but so do agencies such as the (falsely named) Centers for Disease Control and Prevention. What was interesting about Trump is that he did not try to hide his ineptitude for the job or for his egoism. The Washington-entrenched try to cover theirs. It is better to see the true face than be blindsided.

"From Trump to Biden to Sanders to Pelosi to most of the US Senate," Krein wrote in June of 2021, "one might think that the biblical three score and ten (70-plus years of age) had become a mandatory minimum for holding office" in the United States of America. For twenty-four of the previous thirty-two years (and by 2024), the United States of America will have been under the leadership of men and women born before the fumes of a world war had dissipated and as new acts of aggression were being instigated.

Joint Houses of the US Congress include the House of Representatives and Senate; their membership total 535 voting officials. The Senate's voting members total 100; the House membership totals 435 (with five delegates, one resident commissioner). US Senate leadership includes the president of the Senate and the Senate majority leadership (president pro tempore, Senate majority leader, Senate majority whip) and the Senate minority leadership (Senate minority leader, Senate minority whip). US House leadership includes the Speaker of the House and the House majority leadership (House majority leader, House majority whip) and the House minority leadership (House minority leader, House minority whip).

Most of these people were no doubt thought to have died long ago as they have not appeared or been referenced in the loudest US media sources. However, all of them are dead or dying, and dangerous to the future of America. They produce nothing of value. It does not matter what their superficial coverings, their tribal coding, or their self-identified ideological bent, these people are the incestuous extremists, the albatross, the stranglehold holding back rational relations, competence and diligence in work, quality service, and substantive progress in US domestic and foreign affairs, which is essential to the current era and to future ages.

US Senate: As of December 2021, these men and women were the obvious gerontocrats: US Senators ages sixty-five and older *(close to half of the one-hundred-member body)*

65
1. Jeff Merkley
2. Jon Tester

66
3. Lindsey Graham
4. Ron Johnson
5. Richard Burr
6. Rob Portman

7. Sheldon Whitehouse

67
8. Tommy Tuberville
9. Mike Braun
10. Jerry Moran
11. Mike Rounds
12. Mark Warner
13. Cynthia Lummis

68
14. Shelley Moore Capito
15. Bob Menendez

69
16. Marsha Blackburn
17. John Cornyn
18. John Barrasso
19. John Hickenlooper

20. Rick Scott

72

32. Jack Reed
33. Elizabeth Warren
34. Ron Wyden

70

23. Mike Crapo
24. John Kennedy
25. Roger Wicker
26. Deb Fischer

73 (0)
76 (0)
74

35. Mitt Romney
36. Joe Manchin
37. Tom Carper
38. Mazie Hirono
39. Jeanne Shaheen

71

27. Roy Blunt
28. Chuck Schumer
29. Patty Murray
30. John Boozman
31. Debbie Stabenow

75

40. Richard Blumenthal

41. Ed Markey

77

42. Angus King
43. Dick Durbin

78

44. Jim Risch
45. Ben Cardin

79

46. Mitch McConnell

80

47. Bernie Sanders

81

48. Patrick Leahy

US House of Representatives: As of January 1, 2022, with two vacancies, the 117th Congress' House of Representatives was composed of 433 voting members. As of December 2021, there were 148 members (roughly 35 percent of the body) aged sixty-five and older seated in the United States House of Representatives. (Age number in bold typed above members' names.)

65

1. Robin Kelly
2. Jesús "Chuy" García
3. Greg Pence
4. Ron Estes
5. Ann McLane Kuster
6. Kathy Manning
7. Bob Latta
8. French Hill
9. Tom McClintock
10. Charlie Crist

66

11. Pete Sessions
12. Henry Cuellar
13. Dan Newhouse
14. Glenn Grothman
15. Gregorio Sablan
16. Michelle Steel
17. Bill Foster
18. Mariannette Miller-Meeks
19. Chellie Pingree
20. David Trone
21. Stephen F. Lynch
22. Billy Long
23. Kevin Brady

67

24. Gary Palmer
25. Brad Sherman
26. Doug Lamborn
27. Carlos Giménez
28. Hank Johnson
29. Brenda Lawrence
30. Betty McCollum
31. Adriano Espaillat
32. Bill Johnson
33. Bob Gibbs
34. Suzanne Bonamici
35. Dwight Evans
36. Jim Cooper
37. Mo Brooks

68

38. Ken Calvert
39. Darrell Issa
40. Ed Perlmutter
41. Joe Courtney
42. Neal Dunn
43. Fred Upton
44. Debbie Dingell
45. Jeff Van Drew
46. Chris Smith
47. Gregory Meeks
48. Nydia Velázquez
49. Steve Chabot
50. Mike Doyle
51. Ralph Norman
52. Louie Gohmert
53. Randy Weber
54. Judy Chu
55. Karen Bass

69

56. Ed Case
57. Bill Keating
58. Blaine Luetkemeyer
59. Cliff Bentz
60. Mark DeSaulnier
61. Jim Costa
62. Julia Brownley
63. John Rutherford

70

64. Tim Walberg
65. Frank Pallone
66. Albio Sires
67. Kurt Schrader
68. Burgess Owens
69. Gwen Moore
70. Mike Thompson
71. Jerry McNerney
72. Vern Buchanan

73. Rick W. Allen

71

74. Joyce Beatty
75. Sheila Jackson Lee
76. Michael C. Burgess
77. Sylvia Garcia
78. Don Beyer
79. Gerry Connolly
80. Carol Miller
81. Ann Kirkpatrick
82. Jackie Speier
83. Mike Simpson
84. Dina Titus

72

85. Steve Cohen
86. Roger Williams
87. Daniel Webster
88. Richard Neal
89. Paul Tonko
90. Tom Cole

73

91. Brian Babin
92. Raúl Grijalva
93. John B. Larson
94. Al Lawson
95. Lois Frankel
96. Kweisi Mfume
97. Bennie Thompson
98. Earl Blumenauer
99. Mike Kelly

74

100. Bobby Scott
101. David McKinley
102. Amata Coleman Radewagen (Delegate)
103. Zoe Lofgren

104. Bill Posey
105. Sanford Bishop
106. John Yarmuth
107. Jack Bergman

108. Jerry Nadler
109. G. K. Butterfield
110. Peter DeFazio
111. Joe Wilson
112. Al Green
113. Peter Welch

75

114. Barbara Lee
115. Bobby Rush
116. Dutch Ruppersberger
117. Carolyn Maloney
118. Alma Adams
119. Marcy Kaptur
120. Lloyd Doggett
121. Tom O'Halleran

76

122. Jim Baird
123. Bonnie Watson Coleman
124. John Garamendi
125. David Scott

77

126. Doris Matsui
127. Jan Schakowsky
128. Emanuel Cleaver

78

129. Virginia Foxx
130. Kay Granger
131. Rosa DeLauro

79

132. Anna Eshoo
133. Frederica Wilson

80

134. Alan Lowenthal
135. Danny K. Davis
136. John Carter
137. Lucille
   Roybal-Allard

81

138. Jim Clyburn
139. Nancy Pelosi
140. David Price

82

141. Steny Hoyer

83

142. Maxine Waters

84

143. Eleanor Holmes
   Norton (Delegate)

144. Hal Rogers
145. Bill Pascrell

85

146. Grace Napolitano

86

147. Eddie Bernice
   Johnson

87 (0)

88

148. Don Young

US House and Senate: The detached super-wealthy ending 2021 included these US House and Senate members (top tier):

- Member US Senate Mark Robert Warner (#1): $214.1 million
- Member US House of Representatives Gregory Richard Gianforte (#1): $189.3 million
- Member US House of Representatives Vernon Gale Buchanan (#6): $157.2 million
- Member US House of Representatives Donald Sternoff Beyer Jr. (#8): $124.9 million

Wealth Ranking Numbers 10–23 in US House and Senate

10. Nancy Patricia Pelosi (US House): $114.7 million
11. John Henry Hoeven III (US Senate): $93.4 million
12. Dianne Goldman Berman Feinstein (US Senate): $87.9 million
13. Suzan Kay DelBene (US House): $79.4 million
14. Frederick Stephen Upton (US House): $79.0 million
15. Ronald Harold Johnson (US Senate): $78.5 million
16. John Roger Williams (US House): $67.0 million
17. Earl Leroy "Buddy" Carter (US House): $66.5 million
18. James Elroy Risch (US Senate): $41.8 million
19. Addison Mitchell McConnell III (US Senate): $34.1 million
20. Steven David Daines (US Senate): $32.9 million

21. Kevin Ray Hern (US House): $61.0 million (2018 estimate)
22. Scott Harvey Peters (US House): $60.5 million (2018 estimate)
23. Richard Wayne Allen (US House): $52.1 million (2018 estimate)

The multilayered crisis of the 2019 *and continuing* pandemic—one of many sectors undergoing crises in the United States—exposes the self-annihilative harm that is being done, in Krein's words, "by a ruling class that is more qualified for long-term care than for holding important and intensely demanding positions."

Yet across the board, from politics to academia to corporate entities' boardrooms and executive suites, gerontocratic institutions and the gerontocratic mind continues to sacrifice readiness for everyone—essential education, skills, and readiness in an age far advanced in globalization—"in order to pad the incomes of septuagenarians who should have retired years ago."

Independent journalist Caitlin Johnstone as characterized the United States as

> a unipolar (gerontocratic) superpower governed by octogenarians who work for corporations and banks where military weapons are made by prison slaves to be launched at impoverished foreigners while celebrities attend lavish galas, and police guard food in dumpsters from the homeless.

Old is as old does. Gerontocrats and kleptocrats prefer the profit-taking of making war.

"War" is an old saw, a song sung often by America's entrenched leaders. But just as "enemies" characteristically are US fabrications, not all of what US leaders call war is war. The term "war" presupposes at least three elements or conditions: (1) a clearly observable prior external offense (or offending entity) met by a defending (the homeland) combatant; (2) *at*

DR. CAROLYN LADELLE BENNETT

least two adversaries or antagonists; and (3) open and declared armed hostile conflict *between states* or *nations*. Such battles have a definite beginning and an ending. None of this applies in what American leaders and media entities characterize as war.

US leaders and public figures and more sinister types are manufacturing "enemies," manufacturing "grievances," and manufacturing a notion of war—victimizing the world's peoples and institutions all the while casting themselves as "victims." What US leaders order or acquiesce to and what US military personnel or mercenaries on contract execute on command and what US debt funds and America's convenient allies contribute to is raw aggression driven by US impunity but lacking any external provocation.

There is no war, only continuous unprovoked callous self-serving destruction of America and other countries. Criminals are getting away with murder and calling it war.

There are United States' aggressors, violent interlopers, illegal transgressors into other peoples' lands, rabid killers acting on orders or acquiescence (wink and nod) of US officials and their convenient allies and contracting mercenaries. There are US merchants of death who are tearing apart other nations and severing the hope and potential and promise of the United States of America.

Militarists, kleptocrats, gerontocrats, nihilists (false patriots) serve only themselves while destroying America's preparedness (i.e., its people's preparedness) for the future, preparedness in work, education, general welfare, leisure, society, community.

The incestuous cabal that is bought, sold, managed, and maintained by sinister sources and for which Americans, distracted by the show and having no real choice, vote for repeatedly (and die for) is the incestuous cabal of men and women who are denying Americans basic rights under the US Constitution and under the international conventions and declarations about which many Americans are unconcerned and ignorant.

The Portuguese political scientist and Yale University professor Nuno P. Monteiro was known for his research in the fields of international relations and security studies, particularly in the area of "unipolarity" and nuclear weaponry. Monteiro observed that, after the collapse of the Soviet Union, the United States assumed inordinate, "unparalleled military power," and the international system became "unipolar."

Hunger for power and use of force are like addictions. Constancy is essential. Maintaining power predominance means waging constant wars; and while military power preponderance may bring benefits to some, it brings harm, *continually*, to many.

Joseph Robinette Biden Jr. was incestuously Washington entrenched (almost fifty years), long before becoming a principal occupant at the White House. But perhaps his greatest wrong as US president (as an old-timer, he should have had the courage to make a correction) was locking step with his predecessors—"continuing Trump administration policies," whose policies had "continued Obama administration policies," Johnstone wrote.

Those rising to the pinnacle of power or apparent power surround themselves with other people and entities vested in and devoted to ensuring compliance with and "support for status quo power structures." Caitlin Johnstone concludes her September 2021 piece "Propaganda Scrambles Our Minds" with these observations:

- Elections in the United States of (*Exceptionalism*) America are fraudulent.
- US "politicians are puppets."
- The dominating species "is driven by the interplay of preceding forces stretching back through … evolutionary history and the origin of the universe."

- "'Self' is an illusion." (But in America, illusory or delusional gerontocrats and kleptocrats go to extremes in violence and nepotism to protect and preserve their illusion).

Propaganda spread by the powerful delivers a surround-sound assault (e.g., CNN's insane 24-7 loop of 9/11 falling towers) on the brain such that it severely warps the minds of Americans. They end up disbelieving common sense, disavowing their own values.

Caveman Aggression and the Coward

Americans' anachronism (backwardness), the decay, holding everyone else back destroys the whole.

The violence at home is as real as American drone strikes against Iraq, Afghanistan, Syria, Pakistan, Somalia, and against other peoples and places; as real as the malicious blocking of international movement of goods and services, thwarting thriving economies and development, trashing institutions, cultures, health, and well-being. Washington sets the example for Americans at home and for those labeled terrorists abroad.

The US presidential parting shot announcing another departure from Afghanistan was another massacre in search of manhood.

Caitlin Johnstone suggested in another piece that the difference between the August 29, 2021, US airstrike and the thousands of US airstrikes devastating millions in US leaders' manufactured theaters of war "is that this one was politicized."

> "The Biden administration ordered the August strike to look tough on terrorism (affirm his manhood as predecessors Obama and Hillary Clinton and Bill and Co had done, *my words*) after (an alleged) Kabul airport attack ..."—amidst an anti-withdrawal frenzy being

whipped up "by plutocratic media entities eager to paint ending aggression … as a *bad* thing that everyone should oppose."

Mass media manipulators providing cover for mass military murder …, journalistic malpractice and negligence "… are as complicit in depraved acts of human butchery… as are aggressors and occupiers firing weapons" (including drones operators miles away). Equally complicit, or even more so, are Washington-ensconced officials barking orders, and usually hiding their hand.

Had news entities properly done their jobs and had proper journalists been allowed to use vast investigative resources to discover and report on US leadership's carnage and its victims over the past twenty years and longer, the world, including the body politic of America, would have at least known the truth—known about all those "victims of murder." Perhaps Americans then would have demanded and made better-informed decisions at the ballot box.

The release of information concerning the August carnage shows that mainstream media organizations can delve into "the validity of US airstrikes." It also lays bare a calculated choice, over these many years, "not to investigate" happenings on the ground, and not to reveal the truth.

Even if there is no *war*—in the objective sense of open and declared armed hostile conflict between or among states or nations, between at least two antagonists, on a battlefield or theater of engagement—the overpowering machinery of US reckless aggression is always on display somewhere, anywhere, all the time. Slaughter pays well the kleptocrats and gerontocrats.

If Americans were making rational choices about leaders; if they were expressing genuine concerns about their country, which of these would concern them more?

A leader labeled by US leaders and their partners a dictator over his own country; or the evident US brand of anachronistic and extortionist leader who dispatches mercenaries around the world to kill and maim the youth of nations and their leaders, heads of household, and women and children? Would Americans choose leaders who randomly abduct, torture, and terrorize people in "dark sites" and imprison and torture others whose reporting or publishing or opinions they disagree with or find embarrassing or uncomfortable. Would Americans prefer leaders who plunder and destroy nations' cultures and health (cause people to languish and die with curable diseases), stymie their economics, impede their development, and starve their people to death?

The second set is the documented *true* record of US leaders (who have simultaneously deserted America and her people). It represents a colossal crime crossing centuries that has intensified and hardened in its callousness and recklessness over at least the past forty years, through seven US presidents; and as of January 2022, through twenty congresses (the 97th through the117[th]).

This is the barbarism of the ancients. It is also a portrait of cowardice.

The American coward manufactures but never serves in his (her) wars, which, strictly speaking, at least in contemporary times, are not wars. The coward misrepresents—labels what is *isn't* and isn't *is*. Abuses of human beings' *universal* rights and breaches of nations' sovereignty are not humanitarian acts but criminal acts, which should be prosecuted by independent tribunals.

The coward sends mothers' sons (and daughters) to kill and die (sometimes by the hand of their colleagues), to suffer irreparable physical and mental injury, to be allowed one day to return home and be welcomed as castoffs (throwaways, disposables)—discarded like stray dogs to profiteering nonprofits who transfer them to adoptive strangers (subject to abuse or abandonment); or consigned directly to public streets and tunnels, hovels and underpasses, or mountain hollows to languish in disgracefully inhumane, unclean, disease-causing and disease-spreading camps, all approved or condoned by the incestuous cabal holding the reins of power: the liberal-conservative-progressive, neo and not (left right center, blue red purple state, individual origin-coded) hyphenated cowards.

It is "for your own good," they say. The violence and destruction, the inhumanity to humanity and nature and to principles and institutions at home and abroad—unspeakable actions—the cowards couch in proclamations of "humanitarianism."

"No cloak of pretended righteousness can lessen the responsibility of those through whom life and human faculties are destroyed," wrote the prolific American author and speaker Helen Adams Keller in the 1930s. "No philanthropy can atone for irreparable wrongs of war."

We should work for the kind of *preparedness* that reorganizes and reconstructs the life of the people "as never before"; that educates "all the people so that they shall hate war"; that prevents "vested interests or greed" from sacrificing "lives to cannons" (missiles, mines, chemical weaponry).

The backwardness, chaos, venality and militarism manifest among America's leaders is mimicked and spread among the masses and displayed throughout major institutions of higher learning.

Anachronism Meets Anarchism
Backwardness Meets Chaos

A lunatic brigade enabled by nonprofit profiteers, professional tribalists, and questionable media organizations are attempting the folly of overthrowing the past.

Tearing down historic statues (debating or adjudicating such folly) is not only a fool's errand and an act of mindless extremism, it is also a grand distraction, a show, a stunt, part of the unending tragedy performed by and for Americans under the leadership of incestuous inmates entrenched in and around Washington, and stretching from New England to the Pacific. One "wing" feeds on the other, meeting in their extreme, making each *of a kind*. History and legacy become not a good to be studied and built upon and made better; but rather to be censored and ripped apart, thus instilling ignorance, deliberate blindness, and inevitable regress.

Americans' tribalism and penchant for segregation or separatism (ghettoes and gates) are both anachronistic and anarchic (backward leaning and chaotic).

The Supreme Court decision of the 1950s decreed that segregation is inherently unequal. Segregation promotes inequality as well as an overall unhealthy splintering of society.

Building on this decision would have been to fund and increase schools of education and ensure properly trained professors to educate and assist with the development, retraining, and in-service training of critically important K-12 schoolteachers to be employed and to replenish teaching as well as support staffs of all schools in America.

As with other vital institutions and critical sectors of American society, this essential readiness, this common defense—as distinct from US leaders' venal and corrupt preoccupation with "readiness" for raw aggression at home and abroad—failed to happen.

America's teacher training colleges (originally normal schools) turned into universities named for businessmen and tax-evading foundations and often headed by out-of-field, inept, color-coded, and otherwise unfit administrators. Curriculum began to focus on churning out MBA's, clever proposal writers, and scripted contract proposals contributive to and procreative of government's incestuous militarism. When needed most, fundamental or general education, particularly teacher training had been disparaged and devalued (*anybody* can teach; those who *can't* resort to teaching).

All kinds of militarist and nonsensical, self-serving and clever proposal-writer curricula were introduced that furthered the splintering of Americans. As the quality and character of public officials and thus public office has declined so has the caliber of America's schoolteachers, professors, administrators, the processes of teaching and learning (and access to these), and the caliber of student (entering and exiting institutions of *higher learning*). The care for and overall quality of student knowledge and essential student skills and abilities have declined. Essential qualities of self-reliance and self-discipline, a capacity for critical thinking, reflective, independent, and rational thought; creativity; an appreciation for lifelong learning—all have been replaced with festering resentment and isolation coupled with dependency and a sense of victimhood (*Poor me*).

Long before the pandemic of 2019, American society was backward trending, splintered and unready, unprepared for present and future.

Splintered and Unready: Americans in the past died to desegregate schools, businesses, places of employment, voting precincts, and neighborhoods. The quest was not to separate from America but to join in contributing to America.

A key achievement known (or should be known) to every American schoolchild is *Brown v. Board of Education*.

Brown v. Board of Education of Topeka was a case in which, on May 17, 1954, the Supreme Court of the United States ruled unanimously (9–0) that racial segregation in public schools violated the Fourteenth Amendment to the Constitution, which prohibits the states from denying equal protection of the laws to any person within their jurisdictions.

Brown rejected the earlier "separate but equal" doctrine (SCOTUS 1896 *Plessy v. Ferguson*) that had maintained the constitutionality of separate public facilities for white and Negro Americans if such facilities were "approximately equal"; and declared that separate educational facilities for white and Negro Americans were inherently unequal. The 1954 decision strictly applied to public schools but *implied that segregation was impermissible in other public facilities.*

Brown is considered one of the most important rulings in the history of the US high court. The American civil rights movement of the late 1950s and 1960s progressed from its standard.

No matter how it is twisted or who does the twisting, segregation remains an extremism that feeds on itself. That embodies and inspires fear and hostility. That promotes inequality and ignorance. That is unchallenged and unchallenging.

Nevertheless, America's Super Ivy Leagues—where the rich can buy acceptance letters, where assassins are bred, and where human traffickers and drug pushers can have wings bearing their names—are billboarding and practicing segregation outright, creating and showing off parallel societies, institutionalizing the ghettoization of America. Like their graduates' *humanitarian* massacres in Iraq, Pakistan, Syria, and Afghanistan, their assassinations in Libya and Haiti, they are telling Americans, *This is good for you.* In America, segregation is severing the Union. These are some of the examples.

- Stanford University's Black Graduation, according to its website, is an annual segregated event "to commemorate the many achievements of Stanford's (black) graduating students with (black) family and friends." Cloaked in humanitarianism, the statement declares the event to be "meant to celebrate the long tradition of cultural awareness at Stanford."
- Harvard University's Black Graduation Ceremony, according to Harvard's website, "honor[s] the academic achievements of

'Black' Harvard graduating students and their (Black) families." "(Black) Registration is required." Separately held is Harvard University's "Latinx Graduation Ceremony" focusing on "the achievements of ('Latinx') students (and) those (presumably 'Latinx' [?]) who helped ('Latinx') students get to and graduate from Harvard."

- Columbia University's segregated affairs according to its website: Lavender Graduation Celebration (LGBTQIA+ community) April 26; Asian Graduation Celebration 10 a.m. April 27; First-Generation and/or Low-Income Community (FLI) Graduation Celebration 7:00 p.m. April 27; Latinx Graduation Celebration April 29; "Black Graduation Celebration" April 30.

Before the high court in *Brown v. Board of Education of Topeka*, the American attorney Thurgood Marshall made the indisputable, compelling argument that "segregation in public education produced unequal schools for Negro *and* white Americans" (emphasis added).

In addition to his legal argument, it is said that Marshall's "reliance on psychological, sociological, and historical data (also) sensitized" the High Court to the "deleterious effects of institutionalized segregation on the self-image, social worth, and social progress of African (Negro) American children."

Thurgood Marshall was no victim, lightweight, or color-coded hire. Before *Brown*, he had a well-established reputation as a counselor before the court. Throughout the 1940s and 1950s, Marshall distinguished himself as one of America's top lawyers. He won twenty-nine of thirty-two cases he argued before the Supreme Court of the United States. The high court's decisions in the 1944 *Smith v. Allwright* case declaring unconstitutional a Southern state's exclusion of Negro American voters from primary elections; the 1948 *Shelley v. Kraemer* case striking down a state court enforcement of a private agreement ("restrictive covenant") to sell real property only to white people; and the 1950 cases *Sweatt v. Painter* and *McLaurin v. Oklahoma State Regents* declaring unconstitutional "separate but equal" facilities for Negro American professionals and graduate students in state universities were part Marshall's portfolio.

During the 200th anniversary celebrations of the Constitution of the United States, Thurgood Marshall spoke in Maui, Hawaii (May 6, 1987), at the annual seminar of a San Francisco law association commemorating anniversary.

Down the long road of history begun in Philadelphia, Marshall said real progress had been advanced by Americans who refused to settle for "outdated notions of 'liberty,' 'justice,' and 'equality.'" These people, he said, "strived to better them."

We must be mindful of "the momentous events" that followed the Constitutional Convention. Instead of merely paying homage to a document now stored in a vault in the National Archives, we must keep a "proper sense of perspective."

Marshall said during that 1987 commemoration that Americans must seek "a sensitive understanding of the Constitution's inherent defects" as well as "its promising evolution through 200 years of history." The miracle at Philadelphia in 1787 was the birth of a living document, "a life (that has been) nurtured through two turbulent centuries of our own making," he said; "a life" that embodies never-before realized or afforded "good fortune."

Jurist Thurgood Marshall, nominated by US president Lyndon Johnson, was an associate justice on the Supreme Court of the United States (1967–1991). Before SCOTUS, he was US solicitor general (1965–1967), and a judge (nominated by President John F. Kennedy) on the US court of appeals for the second circuit. Marshall was an accomplished American lawyer, a civil rights activist, and jurist born in Baltimore, Maryland, on July 2, 1908. He died in Bethesda, Maryland, January 24, 1993.

It is possible that, in later times, Marshall would have disagreed with current actions taken by US Ivy Leagues. Perhaps he would have agreed, to some extent, with Denmark's de-ghettoization efforts.

Denmark seems to have taken opposition to a corrosive element in society—a phenomenon that Americans protested in the past, appeared to have triumphed over in the twentieth century, only to regress to in the twenty-first century.

The Denmark case is really a double consequence of US aggression that has raged relentlessly across Western Asia, was worsened by the US (hysterical Hillary Clinton / African-parentage Barack Obama's) assassination of Libya's head of state and the decimation of the country's government-provided breakwater that held back the tsunami of people forced to flee their African and Asian homelands.

Some Denmark officials fear and have attempted to excise the resulting "parallel societies" or "ghettoes" cropping up in their country. It may be a hard sell for the Danes. To some natives and distant observers, it seems to be a harsh and heartless move. But ghettoes are unhealthy for any general society. The Danes have defined ghetto as a housing area comprised of more than one thousand inhabitants, 50 percent (or more) of whom are of "non-Western nationality or heritage;" and where two of four additional criteria apply, criteria such as employment, heritage, crime rate, education, and income.

Denmark's "ghetto list" was reported to have originated in 2010 and was later introduced, in 2018, as "ghetto plan" legislation. The reasoning used by Danish officials "to combat the ghettoization of 'vulnerable' areas" was that

> high concentrations of foreigners living in residential areas increase the risk that distinct 'religious and cultural parallel societies' will emerge.

The Ministry of Interior proposed legislation that would limit the number of residents of "non-Western origin" to 30 percent in any given neighborhood. The law would go into effect over a ten-year period.

The Denmark case is particularly relevant in light of the US situation and Americans' backward and anarchistic tendencies and because the ghetto phenomenon and its consequences have long been ignored in the United States. But no matter where they are or how they are constructed, ghettoes perpetuate unhealthy isolation and militate against human understanding. They create and perpetuate inequality, prejudice and paranoia. They break down whole societies and sever the unity of individual nations. Denmark may need to tone down its rhetoric and make alterations in its approach, but the concern is a genuine one that needs attention to originating factors, to current situations, and to consequences of each reality.

Born Free *not to be* Tribal

The fight for legitimate rights—to participate in choosing leaders, to prepare oneself at the highest levels of learning, skill and achievement, enabling a wide variety of life choices and contribution—was a fight to join the Union thoroughly and completely: to be included as a equal part, not segregated as outcasts or terminal victims. Thurgood Marshall never thought of himself as anything but American. All those American civil rights workers and Woman Suffrage workers were American in spirit and to the bone. Never did they think of themselves or identify themselves as "African" or anything other than American.

From its original colonies' independence from the king through the framing of its government, America was conceived as one—the States United in America, not in the tribal lands of Europe and Arabia (Asia and Africa). Call it an "experiment," if you will, but the ideal conceived by the founders of this nation is still worth pursuing and enhancing.

The colossal error down through American history, particularly evident in the postwar years, has been not so much the flaw in the founding discussions and documents, not in the legacy left by the founders but in the unfitness for purpose of leaders—often panderers and corruptible men and women on the payroll of private interests—distanced from the founding. The shallowness, shortsightedness, weakness, superficiality of the later generations of American leaders and their failure to debate and deliberate in good faith on behalf of the nation has led to America's backwardness and its breakdown.

Their failure to take the beginning and the legacy, the promise and potential and, in studied diligence, not in build-"*back*" or make-"*again*" backwardness but, rather, make the beginning better, the gift improved—the forming of a "more perfect Union" a demonstrable pledge and practice.

Vocal Americans, in various media and government today, seem to want to be something other than *American*. Even among those who boast most of being American, perhaps flying an American flag on their front porches or attaching one to their big vehicles, present themselves as hyphenations (African, German, Irish, Italian, Latin, Polish, Jewish/ Catholic/Christian) with "American" rendered an afterthought (a mongrel no one really wants to be); a sign that sends America's principled founders and the nineteenth century crusaders for legitimate rights spinning in their graves.

Perhaps the average American does not think of women as among the great founders of America; but there were women founders, at least in my view. They were among the makers of a more perfect Union. There was something magnificent, substantively wonderful in women born in the nineteenth and late eighteenth centuries that no woman graduating from today's Ivy Leagues has matched. If today's performances and the accolades given to the Hillary Clintons and tenured university professors spouting expletives are any indication, perhaps contemporary Americans prefer ignorance and dissociation from America's forbears

DR. CAROLYN LADELLE BENNETT

and their true greatness. For a later book, I have been thinking about early American women whom today's young women would do well to study and perhaps emulate.

Early American Women Crusaders for Life, Education, and Inclusion

- Northerner (New England) Lucretia Coffin Mott: abolitionist, suffragist, public speaker, teacher; lifetime: January 3, 1793 – November 11, 1880

- Southerner (Deep South) Angelina Emily Grimké, (Weld): abolitionist, suffragist, public speaker; lifetime: February 20, 1805 – October 26, 1879

- Northerner (Middle Atlantic) Jane Grey Cannon Swisshelm: abolitionist, nurse in military hospitals, suffragist, journalist and publisher, public speaker, teacher; lifetime: December 6, 1815 – July 22, 1884

- Southerner (South Atlantic) Harriet Tubman (b. Araminta Ross): abolitionist, Civil War spy and nurse, suffragist; lifetime: circa March 1822 – March 10, 1913

- Southerner (South Atlantic) Mary Ann Shadd Cary: abolitionist, journalist and publisher, educator; lifetime: October 9, 1823 – June 5, 1893

- Midwesterner Carrie Lane Chapman Catt: crusader for peace and woman suffrage; lifetime: January 9, 1859 – March 9, 1947

- Midwesterner Laura Jane Addams: crusader for social and political rights, and against war; lifetime: September 6, 1860 – May 21, 1935.

- Southerner (Deep South) Ida Bell Wells Barnett: woman suffragist, crusader against lynching, journalist and publisher, teacher, public speaker, organizer; lifetime: July 16, 1862-March 25, 1931

- Southerner (Deep South) Mary McLeod Bethune: social and political activist, newspaper columnist, educator; lifetime: July 10, 1875- May 18, 1955

- Northerner (Middle Atlantic) Anna Eleanor Roosevelt: social and political activist, diplomat, newspaper columnist and broadcaster; lifetime: October 11, 1884-November 7, 1962

No doubt many Americans may call to mind other American women (and men) who fit into the category of Americans who cared enough about America to crusade for betterment; and, by their deeds, demonstrated their pride in being non tribal—simply American.

Not long ago, I read a thoroughly believable expression of allegiance that is rarely heard with equal believability from contemporary Americans. It was uttered by a leader whom US leaders and partners choose to label "enemy." He said, "I can tell you that my love of (country) ... has increased masses of times over the years ... and I am not afraid to express myself in such a way.... I am Russian. My roots are in Russia. My ancestors lived for 300 years in the same village and went to the same church .... Knowing this is exciting. I feel a part of our country and a part of the Russian people...." In this expression is no hedging or hesitancy; no uncertainty or hyphenation.

In another context, speaking of the Russian Federation and what comprises and sustains Union, President Vladimir Putin said something else that zeroes in on the vital importance of shared language, culture, values, the history and traditions of and loyalty to one's country. "This is everything," he said, "that unites our people around common ideals and determines the vector for the development of the sovereign, independent and peace-loving Russian state, an active member of the international community." The character and content of policy relations with other nations must ensure, he said, "the most comfortable and secure conditions" for domestic "development, resolving ambitious socioeconomic tasks and improving the living standards of our people."

The Russian President seems to feel no psychological breach or brain split. One (*a true patriot*) can love one's own country and not hate or disparage other countries, leaders, and peoples; or seek to dominate, suppress, or destroy them.

In the United States, government leaders and public figures, so intent on serving themselves, have broken the connection with and among the American people. They have created deep divisions, instilled distrust, and discouraged the essential (felt) connection between the people and their country. Leaders have broken faith with the people; and in doing so, they have broken the nation.

Earlier presidents, who followed Lincoln and preceded the contemporary crop of leaders, had urged care of America's Union. They warned against violence and fear and want. One example was in content used by President Franklin Delano Roosevelt. In 1941, the thirty-second US president put forth a vision that he described as "no vision of a *distant* millennium (but) ... a definite basis for a kind of world attainable in our own time and generation" (emphasis added). Roosevelt envisioned a world founded on four essential human freedoms:

- Freedom of speech and expression *(not recklessness)*
- Freedom of every person to worship God in his own way *(not have a deity or religious dogma imposed by government officials and their partners)*
- Freedom from want (translated into world terms means economic understandings that secure to all nations, *not one nation*, a healthy peacetime existence for all inhabitants).
- Freedom from fear (translated into world terms means reduction of armaments worldwide to such a point and in such a thorough fashion that no nation will be in a position to commit acts of

physical aggression against other nations; it means ending the demonization and slanderous propaganda that forms the basis of bad policy decisions in domestic and international affairs, sustains fear, and worsens paranoia)

Dwight David Eisenhower, America's thirty-fourth president, warned of an American propensity for self-inflicted harm and its disastrous consequences. "We must avoid the impulse to live only for today," Eisenhower said. The combined colossus of military establishment and arms industry portends "grave" consequences; and "we must never let the weight of this combination endanger our liberties or democratic processes." A responsible (alert and knowledgeable) citizenry must "compel the proper meshing of the huge industrial and military machinery of defense with our peaceful methods and goals, so that security and liberty may prosper together." Responsible government "must guard against the acquisition of unwarranted influence, whether sought or unsought, by the military-industrial complex."

Unfortunately, America's contemporary leaders have thrived on violence and on people's fear and want, thrived on weakness in the people and in America's essential institutions—including the institution of government. Carelessly and cavalierly, these leaders have breached the Union.

In the general population and in mass media, America's founding principles have been misrepresented and misused, trivialized and delegitimized (like the American flag frayed, dragging in the dirt of a "patriot's" car dealership). False patriots have shown themselves to be blind to America's potential and unconscious of the citizenry's responsibility in fulfilling that potential. Leaders and the public at large have squandered the legacy of America's founding men and women.

1

Part 2 Global Hostility

World, Domestic News Evidence of Anachronism

ACTUAL WAR IS an officially declared act comprised of at least two combatants in battle in a clearly defined theater of action, with a clearly defined beginning and ending. However, the hostilities being legislated and ordered, often capriciously, by US leaders and their partners and conducted under their command (or by acquiescence) all over the world are not wars but acts and policies of criminal aggression against sovereign states, lands, and peoples.

To do its bidding, the US cabal bullies, bribes, contracts, and deploys a multitude of convenient allies, North Atlantic stooges and regional commands; and, in one way or another, traffics in and deploys lethal weaponry; disease-causing deprivation and destabilization agents and conglomerates, corrupt nationals, and armed "peacekeepers" (a contradiction in terms), "nongovernmental," "religious," and "terrorist" groups making them partners in a colossal and continuous criminal undertaking against peoples and sovereignties—indeed *against all of nature.*

In conditions of malfeasance unchecked by law, the prevailing scheme undermines not only international law and order but the Constitution of the United States. It prevents basic domestic preparedness, impairs the health and welfare of the American people, and weakens their overall constitution.

The US cabal comprised of major media and academic-mercenary-nonprofit complexes together with government officials and politicians revolving in and out of government, using major platforms to aid, abet, and propagandize war should be outlawed and dismantled, prosecuted, and held to account before an independent, world tribunal.

World news headlines, information, and commentary not mainstreamed in the United States tell the story far more succinctly and compellingly than any other narrative form.

Manufactured Enemies

Robinson, Paul. "Nobody can ever hate Russia enough to satisfy West's fanatical anti-Moscow fringe, as mainstream commentators are now discovering." RT opinion. May 15, 2021. https://www.rt.com/russia/523816-fanatical-anti-kremlin-hatred/

Lindorff, Dave. "US beyond shameless in decrying Belarus' forcing down of passenger plane to nab journalist critic: Recall the tale of Bolivia President Morales' plane in 2013?" Nation of Change. May 25, 2021. https://www.nationofchange.org/2021/05/25/us-beyond-shameless-in-decrying-belarus-forcing-down-of-passenger-plane-to-nab-journalist-critic/

> "The moral standing of the US has been (abysmal) for decades." And the "latest US official expression of indignation over the Lukashenko outrage moves the US out of the abyss and into the gutter."

Koo, George. "One man's view of an 'Upside-Down World': Clyde Prestowitz's latest work is a worthy read, but has some serious flaws." *Asia Times*. April 26, 2021. https://asiatimes.com/2021/04/one-mans-view-of-an-upside-down-world/

When the folks in Washington call out 'communist' China, it says it all. This epithet justifies all the bad things we can ascribe to that country — even when China has systematically lifted millions out of poverty every year ....

The United States deploys around the world some "800 to 1,000 military bases"; yet US leaders and other public figures with microphones or an Internet connection "get upset and alarmed" because China may have two such bases. ...

"Overlooked in such recriminations is that China simply does not play by the same rules as the United States.

"China has never acted on or expressed the desire to become the world's No 1 military power. Its most powerful diplomatic tool is the 'Belt and Road Initiative' to help other countries build their infrastructure."[2]

"'Chinese debt trap' rhetoric an attempt to mislead world through kindergarten mathematics." Xinhua. May 19, 2021. http://www.xinhuanet.com/english/2021-05/19/c_139956630.htm

"US uses dollar to wage economic, political war, says Putin." Press TV news. June 5, 2021. https://www.presstv.com/Detail/2021/06/05/658301/Russia-President-Vladimir-Putin-US-dollar-tool-to-wage-economic-war

Diesen, Glenn analysis. "The real 'malign influence'? How America helped destroy democracy and turn Ukraine's Maidan [Maidan Nezalezhnosti (Independence Square), Kyiv] dream into a nightmare

---

[2] George Koo is the founder and former managing director of International Strategic Alliances.

for its people." RT news May 18, 2021https://www.rt.com/russia/524034-america-destroy-democracy-ukraine/[3]

Nader, Ralph. "Biden: End Your Co-Belligerent Backing of Israeli War Crimes." *Nader* blog. May 21, 2021.https://nader.org/2021/05/21/biden-end-your-co-belligerent-backing-of-israeli-war-crimes/

"Pentagon Special Forces nominee says US should 'strongly consider' training Taiwanese guerillas against 'Chinese invasion.'" RT news May 29, 2021. https://www.rt.com/usa/525135-pentagon-nominee-taiwan-guerillas/

"Biden pursuing 'hubristic, hyper-nationalist imperialist foreign policy': Scholar." Press TV. April 30, 2021. https://www.presstv.com/Detail/2021/04/30/651645/Biden-pursuing-%E2%80%98hubristic,-hyper-nationalist-imperialist-foreign-policy%E2%80%99

Tickle, Jonny. "Washington rejected Moscow's offer of complete reset in Russia-US relations shortly after inauguration of [US President Joseph] Biden—Foreign Minister Lavrov reveals." RT news. April 28, 2021. https://www.rt.com/russia/522343-lavrov-us-rejects-better-relations/

> The Kremlin proposed a complete reset in the strained relationship between Moscow and Washington after the inauguration of US President Joe Biden, but it was turned down by the White House, Russia's chief diplomat said on Tuesday.

"US imposes new sanctions against Russia, expels ten diplomats & targets national debt in move Moscow may view as major escalation" RT news. April 15, 2021. https://www.rt.com/russia/521127-us-sanctions-new-round/

---

[3] Glenn Diesen is a University of South-Eastern Norway Professor.

> US President Joe Biden signed a decree on [April 15, 2021] imposing a new round of sanctions on Russia. They target more than 30 individuals and organizations. The White House also moved to expel nearly a dozen of Moscow's diplomats.

Robinson, Paul. "Biden's Russia policy ludicrous, unbelievable, contradictory & unprecedented: First offers Putin summit & then imposes sanctions." RT news. April 15, 2021. https://www.rt.com/russia/521101-biden-putin-policy-rethink/[4]

"US military contractor announces exit from Iraq amid growing attacks." Press TV. May11, 2011. https://www.presstv.com/Detail/2021/05/11/652451/US-Lockheed-Martin-Iraq

Cloughley, Brian. "Forget the Starving Children in Afghanistan and Intensify Anti-China Provocation." Strategic Culture Foundation. August 31, 2021. https://www.strategic-culture.org/news/2021/08/31/forget-the-starving-children-in-afghanistan-and-intensify-anti-china-provocation/[5]

"Is China the Enemy? History, Context, Development-Part II." Peace Pivot. Brian Becker and K. J. Noh conversation. https://peacepivot.org/interview-with-kj-noh/

> The Anti-China Narrative: the Escalation for War" represents "full-scale animus." US policy has undergone a "geostrategic shift," a "reorientation of US military and foreign policy (again)." The policy "now targets

---

[4] Paul Robinson is a professor at the University of Ottawa who writes about Russian and Soviet history, military history, and military ethics. His blog is *Irrussianality*.
[5] Brian Cloughley is an Australian and British military veteran, a former deputy head of the UN military mission in Kashmir, and former Australian defense attaché in Pakistan.

China as an 'enemy,' instead of "a mix of … cooperative country and … competitor."

ANSWER Coalition National Director Brian Becker has been quoted saying that regarding Asia, "the principle goal" of US administrations has been "to secure US hegemony" by "blocking the economic and diplomatic rise of China.

> Whereas Barack Obama spoke of a "pivot to Asia" …, the vice president in the Trump administration [Michael Pence] spoke of an 'Indo-Pacific' strategy; and on his visits to Singapore and Papua New Guinea, he tried to stir up anti-Chinese sentiment among members of the Association of Southeast Asian Nations (ASEAN) and Asia-Pacific Economic Cooperation (APEC)….

> In the event of a conflict, the United States will certainly press unaligned nations … to take sides, a situation that can only come to their detriment…." (Source Key Wiki) https://keywiki.org/Brian_Becker https://keywiki.org/Brian_Becker#China.27s_Great_Road

Continuous Policies and Practice of Aggression[6,7,8,9]

"Authorization for Use of Military Force" (AUMF): Public Law 107–40 introduced in the US Senate (S.J. Res.23) by Thomas Andrew "Tom" Daschle (D–SD) September 14, 2001; passed in the Senate September 14, 2001 (98–0); passed in the US House of Representatives (H.J.Res.64) September 14, 2001 (420–1); signed into law by President George W. Bush September 18, 2001.

https://en.wikipedia.org/wiki/Authorization_for_Use_of_Military_Force_of_2001

Orlov, Dmitry. "Killing for the Sake of It: The Grisly Reality of the Failing US Empire" article first published 2015, republished September 1, 2021 https://russia-insider.com/en/military/killing-sake-it-grisly-reality-failing-us-empire/ri5200

---

[6] US Secretary of Defense Lloyd James Austin III spent a career in US foreign and Washington public sector military positions. On hiatus, he joined the board of directors of the military contractor Raytheon Technologies (his stock holdings estimated in 2020 at half a million dollars plus compensation totaling $2.7 million). In December 2020, President-elect Joseph Biden nominated Austin for US Secretary of Defense, and by a vote of 93-2, the US Senate in January 2021 signed off on the nomination. Biden also had nominated Washington and defense insider Antony John Blinken for US Secretary of State, and the US Senate confirmed Blinken in January by a vote of 78–22. The two insiders had been operatives in the Biden presidential campaign and on his transition team. Along with former Pentagon advisor, Michele Flournoy, Austin and Blinken also had been partners of Pine Island Capital Partners (a strategic partner of WestExec), "a private equity firm investing in defense companies that touted its access to Washington."

[7] Alyce McFadden "Dept of Defense: Secretary of Defense Lloyd Austin biography" Open Secrets updated March 9, 2021 https://www.opensecrets.org/revolving/rev_summary.php?id=82688

[8] "Lloyd Austin," Wikipedia Foundation, updated June 28, 2022, https://en.wikipedia.org/wiki/Lloyd_Austin

[9] "Antony Blinken," Wikipedia Foundation, updated June 19, 2022, https://en.wikipedia.org/wiki/Antony_Blinken

Siddique, Ashik. "COVID Shrank the Global Economy, but US Military Spending is Still More Than Next 11 Countries Combined." National Priorities. April 28, 2021 https://www.nationalpriorities.org/blog/2021/04/28/us-now-spends-more-military-next-11-countries-combined/

Koshgarian, Lindsay. "The Pentagon Increase Is the Size of the Entire CDC Budget." National Priorities May 14, 2021 https://www.nationalpriorities.org/blog/2021/05/14/pentagon-increase-size-entire-cdc-budget/

"'So proud to have a woman justifying mass murder!' Secretary of State Blinken roasted for calling Albright [former William Jefferson Blythe Clinton-era secretary of state and representative to the United Nations, Madeleine Albright] his role model" RT news March 28, 2021 https://www.rt.com/usa/519407-albright-role-model-blinken/

> Albright is remembered by the world for telling a Sixty Minutes interviewer that US aggression, the "deaths of half a million Iraqi children, allegedly caused by US sanctions, was 'worth it.'"

"Lavrov slams West's attempts to usurp global decision-making as harmful: Faced with the inability to impose their unilateral or bloc priorities on other countries within the United Nations, Western leading nations are seeking to reverse the process of building a polycentric world says Russia's top diplomat" TASS. May 7, 2021 https://tass.com/politics/1287477

US Department of Defense. "The Department of Defense Releases the President's Fiscal Year 2022 Defense Budget" Statement by Secretary of Defense Lloyd J. Austin III on the President's Fiscal Year 2022 Budget. May 28, 2021 https://www.defense.gov/Newsroom/Releases/Release/Article/2638711/the-department-of-defense-releases-the-presidents-fiscal-year-2022-defense-budg/

Department of Defense "Members of the House Armed Services Committee have voted for a $23.9 billion increase in the defense budget request." September 2021. https://breakingdefense.com/2021/09/hasc-votes-to-increase-defense-budget-by-23-9-billion/

Arms Control. "The administration is requesting about $15.5 billion for nuclear weapons activities at the NNSA in 2022, an increase of $139 million above the 2021 level appropriated by Congress" https://www.armscontrol.org/act/2021-09/news/pentagon-raises-concerns-about-nnsa-budget

The "National Nuclear Security Administration," established by the US Congress in the year 2000, is described on their official website as a "semi-autonomous agency" of the US Department of Energy whose tasks include

"Enhancing national security through the military application of nuclear science;"

Maintaining and enhancing "the safety, security, and effectiveness of the US nuclear weapons stockpile;"

Working "to reduce the global danger from weapons of mass destruction" [contradictory assertion: *making weapons of mass destruction reduces danger of weapons of mass destruction*];

Providing "the US Navy with safe and militarily effective nuclear propulsion;" and

[*Having created the sources of nuclear and radiological emergencies*] responding "to nuclear and radiological emergencies in the United States and abroad."

https://www.energy.gov/nnsa/about-nnsa

"Congressman 'Rambo' (?) GOP lawmaker tried to take helicopter into Afghanistan as part of rogue evacuation mission – reports." RT news September 1, 2021 https://www.rt.com/usa/533590-oklahoma-congressman-mullin-afghanistan-evacuation/

"US House approves $1 billion for Israel's 'Iron Dome' missile system." Press TV news September 23, 2021 https://www.presstv.ir/Detail/2021/09/23/667145/US-House-Israel-Iron-Dome-missile-system

Eaves, Elisabeth. "Why is America getting a new $100 billion nuclear weapon?" *The Bulletin*.

February 8, 2021. https://thebulletin.org/2021/02/why-is-america-getting-a-new-100-billion-nuclear-weapon/

Arizmendi, Anahi. "Haiti in the Crosshairs of a 'Humanitarian Occupation.'" *Orinoco Tribune*. July 28, 2021 https://orinocotribune.com/haiti-in-the-crosshairs-of-a-humanitarian-occupation/.

"US violence keeps targeting Iranians," said Iran's Foreign Minister Mohammad Javad Zarif on the anniversary of an unconscionable atrocity—'the US's downing of an Iranian passenger plane.'"

Press TV news. July 3, 2021. https://www.presstv.ir/Detail/2021/07/03/661462/Iran-United-States-downing-passenger-plane-anniversary-Zarif

"Defense Department Announces $150 Million in Assistance for Ukraine" US Department of Defense press release June 11, 2021 https://www.defense.gov/Newsroom/Releases/Release/Article/2655569/defense-department-announces-150-million-in-assistance-for-ukraine/source/GovDelivery/[10]

---

[10] "Statement by President Joe Biden on Additional Security Assistance to Ukraine," White House Statements and Releases June 1, 2022 [the President]: "Thanks to the additional funding for Ukraine, passed with overwhelmingly bipartisan support in the US Congress, the United States will be able to keep providing Ukraine with more of the weapons …. This new package will arm them with new capabilities and advanced

"Ahead of crucial Putin-Biden summit, Washington raises stakes by announcing $150 million in additional military aid for Ukraine." RT news. June 12, 2021 https://www.rt.com/russia/526370-pentagon-military-aid-ukraine/

"NATO meddles in Russia-Belarus affairs to prevent their integration—diplomat

Russian Foreign Ministry Spokeswoman Maria Zakharova commented on a statement of NATO Secretary-General Jens Stoltenberg." TASS June 6, 2021. https://tass.com/politics/1299567

"US Imposes Sanctions on Syria; Iran vows economic support." Press TV news. July 28, 2021.

https://www.presstv.ir/Detail/2021/07/28/663264/Iran-Syria-economic-partnership-US-sanctions

"US deploys more F-16 warplanes to major Saudi air base." Press TV news. July 21, 2021. https://www.presstv.ir/Detail/2021/07/21/662764/US-deploys-fighter-jets-Saudi-air-base

"Minister of tourism denounces measures against Cuba" News in America dot com, Periodico Digital: of Central America and the Caribbean, MRInternacional S.A. July 21, 2021

https://newsinamerica.com/en/travel/2021/minister-of-tourism-denounces-measures-against-cuba/

Cuba's Minister of Tourism Juan Carlos Garcia said that over a two-year period (2020-2021), "the US blockade against Cuba had caused losses to tourism" (e.g., in

---

weaponry, including HIMARS [Lockheed Martin Missiles & Fire Control manufactured M142 High Mobility Artillery Rocket System] with battlefield munitions...," https://www.whitehouse.gov/briefing-room/statements-releases/2022/06/01/statement-by-president-joe-biden-on-additional-security-assistance-to-ukraine-2/

travel, services, operations and logistics, insurance) estimated at $367,304,825 million."

"The Real Role of NGOs in Venezuela." *Orinoco Tribune*. July 7, 2021. https://orinocotribune.com/?s=Foro+Penal

https://orinocotribune.com/the-real-role-of-ngos-in-venezuela/

Jimenez, Daniela. "What is Behind Arrest of Javier Tarazona from NGO Fundaredes?" *Orinoco Tribune* (RedRadioVE) by Translation *Orinoco Tribune* OT/JRE/SL. July 5, 2021. https://orinocotribune.com/what-is-behind-arrest-of-javier-tarazona-from-ngo-fundaredes/

"Director of NGO Fundaredes Charged with Terrorism" Translation: Orinoco Tribune OT/GMS/SC *Orinoco Tribune*. July 7, 2021. https://orinocotribune.com/director-of-ngo-fundaredes-charged-with-terrorism/

"'We will do this again': US learnt no lesson from Afghan war as govt swept failures under the rug, watchdog warns." RT news July 30, 2021 https://www.rt.com/usa/530639-afghan-war-watchdog-lessons/

"Fact: Biden Plans to Continue Bombing Afghanistan." IPA News Release July 9, 2021 https://accuracy.org/release/fact-biden-plans-to-continue-bombing-afghanistan/

> Institute for Public Accuracy: "On July 6, 2021, Pentagon Press Secretary John Kirby was asked for examples of continued military operations (in Afghanistan).
>
> He responded: 'the way you've seen it being conducted in the past, through— through airstrikes.'"

"Senior official (says) US taking no practical step to promote peace in Yemen." Press TV news. June 28, 2021. https://www.presstv.ir/Detail/2021/06/28/661097/Yemen-US-peace

"Repercussions of the War on Terror in Somalia." *The Global Herald.* September 23, 2021. https://theglobalherald.com/news/repercussions-of-the-war-on-terror-in-somalia/

Brown University Watson Institute of International and Public Affairs "Costs of War update July and September 2021" https://watson.brown.edu/costsofwar/

https://watson.brown.edu/costsofwar/figures/2021/WarDeathToll

Human Costs of Post-9/11 Wars update posted September 1, 2021 (estimates, not including all US "war" zones and theaters of violence): 897,000-929,000 Direct War Deaths in Major War Zones

- Afghanistan and Pakistan (October 2001–August. 2021)
- Iraq (March 2003–August 2021)
- Syria (September 2014–May 2021)
- Yemen (October 2002-August 2021)
- Other Post-9/11 war zones

"The Long-Term Costs of United States Care for Veterans of the Afghanistan and Iraq Wars." Paper. https://watson.brown.edu/costsofwar/papers/2021/CareforVeterans

"High Suicide Rates among United States Service Members and Veterans of the Post-9/11 Wars." Costs of war Project report. June 21, 2021. https://watson.brown.edu/costsofwar/papers/2021/Suicides

https://watson.brown.edu/costsofwar/

"4 times as many US soldiers and vets died by suicide than in combat since 9/11 War on Terror – study." RT news. June 22, 2021 https://www.rt.com/usa/527233-us-military-suicides-study/

"[T]he forever wars launched by the US after 9/11 have led to a surge in military suicides, traumatized soldiers taking their lives as they are repeatedly deployed in conflicts that have no public support."

Costs of War July 2021 update (Veterans):

Monetary cost of caring for post-9/11 war veterans, by 2050, $2.2 to $2.5 trillion

More than 40 percent of post-9/11 (War) veterans— an extraordinarily high proportion – are entitled to lifetime disability payments. This number is expected to increase to 54 percent over the next 30 years.

By comparison, fewer than 25 percent of veterans from World War II, Korea, Vietnam and the first Gulf War have been certified as having a service-connected disability.

The Costs of War Report "recommends the establishment of a Veterans Trust Fund to track and set aside the needed funding for the long-term care of post 9/11 veterans.

Costs of War (Debt: Economic Costs) July 2021 update Post-9/11 wars in Afghanistan, Pakistan, Iraq, and elsewhere https://watson.brown. edu/costsofwar/costs/economic

$6.4 trillion spent or obligated by men and women in Federal Washington through FY 2020: "current wars being 'paid for' almost entirely by borrowing— borrowing that has raised the US budget deficit, increased the national debt, and had other macroeconomic effects such as raising consumer interest rates.

Interest payments estimated by the 2050s "could total more than $6.5 trillion."

- Expenditure (debt) on wars robs from and impoverishes America's people, economy, and institutions—areas such as health and education services and improvements, civilian living-wage jobs, "investment in nonmilitary public infrastructure such as roads and schools."

- Post-9/11 wars "have cost billions of dollars of state, municipal, and private funds, including dollars spent on services for returned veterans and their families and local homeland security efforts."

Costs of War (Social costs update July 2021) https://watson.brown.edu/costsofwar/costs/social

- Post-9/11 wars brought war zones home, rendered Americans "the enemy": militarized policing, sinister surveillance, and selective profiling spread across the nation.

- US legislation and intelligence practices breached constitutional rights, rights to privacy, right to be left alone

- US practice of torture and other mistreatment increased as did detention without end; without counsel, privacy, charge or trial; without right of discovery, and right to bring evidence before an impartial tribunal

- US tax cuts amid enormous debt also drove inequality.

"Millions of Americans lose all unemployment benefits" TV news (Source: AP) Press TV. September 5, 2021 https://www.presstv.ir/Detail/2021/09/05/665918/Millions-of-Americans-lose-all-unemployment-benefits

Alexandrov, Nick. "US Government Turns Somalia into Failed State to Steal Its Oil." "Bombing Somali civilians is one of AFRICOM's main projects," writes Mohamed Haji Ingiriis, a young Somali historian." *Black Agenda Report*. March 24, 2021 https://www.blackagendareport.com/us-government-turns-somalia-failed-state-steal-its-oil

MacDonald, Bryan. "NATO expansion into Ukraine would 'cross red lines' & force Russia and Belarus to act, Kremlin says after Putin-Lukashenko summit." RT news. September 27, 2021

https://www.rt.com/russia/535960-nato-ukraine-red-lines/

> Russia and Belarus have both agreed to "take action" to secure the security of both countries if there were to be any expansion of NATO infrastructure into neighboring Ukraine (Kremlin).

"Japan protests after US Marines dump toxic water in Okinawa sewer…: The government has filed a strong protest with US forces based in Okinawa Prefecture for dumping treated water containing dangerous chemicals into the local sewage system." *Japan Times*. September 4, 2021

https://www.japantimes.co.jp/news/2021/08/29/national/japan-protests-u-s-marines-toxic-water/

Purkiss, Jessica. "Families paying the price for the war in Afghanistan." *The Bureau of Investigative Journalism* June 3, 2020. https://www.thebureauinvestigates.com/stories/2020-06-03/the-families-paying-the-price-for-the-war-in-afghanistan

Afghanistan casualties 2001–2020 Icasualties
Iraq Fatalities Total: 4,899, http://www.icasualties.org/App/Fatalities
Afghanistan Fatalities Total: 3574, http://www.icasualties.org/App/AfghanFatalities

United States Veterans – Pentagon estimated Traumatic brain injuries (TBI) 360,000 US veterans of US aggression in Iraq and Afghanistan of which 45,000 to 90,000 manifest "persistent symptoms requiring specialized care"

People of Iraq (2003–2009)
Iraqi academics frequently threatened with violence, kidnapped, or murdered.
Forty percent (estimated) of Iraq's middle class has fled their homeland (Wikipedia)

People of Afghanistan (2009–2020)
"More than 100,000 Afghans have been killed or wounded" (United Nations Assistance Mission in Afghanistan began documenting these casualties in 2009) *Al Jazeera News* February 2020 https://www.aljazeera.com/indepth/interactive/2020/02/war-afghanistan-2001-invasion-2020-taliban-deal-200229142658305.html

"War robbing Afghanistan of prosperous future, say Baghlan radio panelists." United Nations Assistance Mission in Afghanistan (UNAMA) news May 29, 2019 https://unama.unmissions.org/war-robbing-afghanistan-prosperous-future-say-baghlan-radio-panellists

> In the past 10 years, the United Nations Assistance Mission in Afghanistan documented more than 32,000 civilians killed, around 60,000 injured.

> In 2018 alone, there were 10,993 civilian casualties. Among those killed were 927 children, the highest recorded number of boys and girls killed in the conflict in a single year.

> In the ten year period, "the impact of the war in Afghanistan has been both wide-ranging and devastating, with the country's northeastern provinces

> suffering some of the deadliest fighting ..., leaving
> behind damaged infrastructure, displacing thousands
> of families.

"NATO 'Deluded' Policies Pose Dangers to Europe, World Peace." *SeeNews*. November 14, 2017 https://seenews.net/world/nato-deluded-policies-pose-dangers-to-europe-world-peace.html

Damon, Andre. "NATO summit threatens China, at US instigation." *World Socialist Web Site*. June 14, 2021. https://www.wsws.org/en/articles/2021/06/15/nato-j15.html

"Iraqi, Afghan translators abandoned to their fates." *The Arab Weekly*. June 4, 2021. https://thearabweekly.com/iraqi-afghan-translators-abandoned-their-fates

> Many of the translators who were essential to the
> US and British presence in Iraq and Afghanistan are
> being abandoned. They and their families are facing a
> dangerous future.

"Perpetrators with unmedicated, untreated brain illnesses behind majority of US mass shootings – study" RT news. June 11, 2021. https://www.rt.com/usa/526293-mass-shooting-psychiatric-disorders-study/

"Daesh merged from US backed opposition and Al Qaeda in Iraq and Syria." Press TV news. July 13, 2021. https://www.presstv.ir/Detail/2021/07/13/662133/Daesh-Al-Qaeda-US-war-on-terror-Syria-Iraq-

"'War on all fronts': US media hype Al Qaeda threats just as Pentagon begins 'pullout' from Afghanistan." RT news. May 1, 2021. https://www.rt.com/usa/522657-afghanistan-pullout-alqaeda-threat/

Clandestine infiltration
Cyber-ops
(Home and Abroad)

Greenwald, Glenn. "Questions about the FBI's Role in 1/6 Are Mocked Because the FBI Shapes Liberal Corporate Media." Greenwald, Substack. June 18, 2021 https://greenwald.substack.com/p/questions-about-the-fbis-role-in

> The FBI has been manufacturing and directing terror
> plots and criminal rings for decades. But now, reverence
> for security state agencies reigns.

Greenwald, Glenn. "FBI Using the Same Fear Tactic From the First War on Terror: Orchestrating its Own Terrorism Plots: Questioning the FBI's role in 1/6 was maligned by corporate media as deranged. But only ignorance about the FBI or a desire to deceive could produce such a reaction." Greenwald, Substack. July 24, 2021. https://greenwald.substack.com/p/fbi-using-the-same-fear-tactic-from Makichuk, Dave. "Pentagon's secret spy army said to be 60,000 strong: Ten times the size of the CIA's clandestine element, the force is reportedly aimed at 'minimizing threats' to US security." *Asia Times*. May 21, 2021. https://asiatimes.com/2021/05/pentagons-secret-army-said-to-be-60000-strong/

"US Military's 6000-troop secret force with operations in US and abroad exposed." Press TV. May 18, 2021. https://www.presstv.com/Detail/2021/05/18/656937/US-US-Military-Secret-Army-Geneva-Conventions-Investigation

"Pentagon uses world's largest 'secret army' of 60,000 undercover operatives to carry out 'domestic & foreign' operations – media" RT news. May 18, 2021 https://www.rt.com/usa/524092-pentagon-secret-undercover-army/

"You met Pegasus, on phones, now meet Toka, on any net connected device." Press TV. August 3, 2021. https://www.presstv.ir/Detail/2021/08/03/663632/Israeli-Spyware-Pegasus-Toka- "US government 'SEIZES' website of Iran's Press TV, two other media outlets." RT news. June 22, 2021. https://www.rt.com/news/527292-us-seizes-iran-presstv-websites/

Zuesse, Eric. "Information-Management in the US Dictatorship." *The Duran.* April 25, 2021. https://theduran.com/information-management-in-the-u-s-dictatorship/

Chemical ops

"The Army Quietly Re-Opens Its Infamous Germ Warfare Lab: The Fort Detrick Laboratory Experiments with Ebola, Plague and Other Deadly Toxins; Anthrax Connection" [inspection report obtained by The Frederick News-Post under a Freedom of Information Act request; large sections redacted] DC Report. April 12, 2019. https://www.dcreport.org/2019/12/04/the-army-quietly-re-opens-its-infamous-germ-warfare-lab/

Fowdy, Tom. "It's no surprise the Covid lab leak theory persists in the US, given its history of biological weapons." RT News Opinion. May 27, 2021 . https://www.rt.com/op-ed/524958-covid-lab-leak-theory-usa/
United States germ warfare materials:

> 1942 (FDR- era): Fort Detrick US biological warfare program begins and is alleged to have been used first "in the Korean War, ironically, against the Chinese."

> 1952: information surfaces that "Chinese soldiers from different cities (were) dying with what appeared to be Anthrax and from uncommon conditions such as encephalitis."

1955–1975 (US Vietnam War): chemical and biological weapons are used with grave implications for the population.

1969 (Richard M. Nixon era): Claims to end biological warfare program (consistent with Geneva Protocol and Biological Weapons Convention) but instead switches branding from offense to defense.

2019–2021: Fort Detrick lab is branded with a history of safety violations and closures of its germ research operations (the latest August 2019 after bio safety breaches involving dangerous pathogens. Early March 2020, a US senator begins to continue and spread a lab-leak theory. Chinese diplomat, politician and deputy director of the Chinese Ministry of Foreign Affairs Information Department, Zhao Lijian, suggests looking to the Fort Detrick lab; USA (exceptionalism) officials are outraged and accuse China of *misinformation;* then–US president Donald Trump and his media cohorts begin beating the "China virus" drum, setting off "wholesale *politicization of the pandemic.*"

Tom Fowdy, therefore, questions whether the persisting accusatory American voices command "the moral high ground" from which to accuse China. "The idea of a lab leak—either in Wuhan or in Maryland— is unsubstantiated and, arguably, nonsensical." But, with good reason, "the thought that a state could act in such a way is… weighing on America's national conscience."

> The scheme of deflection and distraction "seeks to represent China as secretive and dangerous, and malevolently plotting against the world by creating pathogens." In reality, it is the United States that "has always done this."

Zhang, Minlu. "WSJ makes false claims on the Wuhan lab leak conspiracy theory" "Some American politicians are again calling for an investigation into the Wuhan lab leak conspiracy theory after the Wall Street Journal published a report in May. A closer look at the report reveals that its statements have no basis." *China Daily*. July 24, 2021. https://www.chinadaily.com.cn/a/202107/24/WS60fb2d36a310efa1bd6640be.html

"OPCW falsified report on staged Douma chemical attack to frame Syria" Press TV news. April 19, 2021. https://www.presstv.com/Detail/2021/04/19/649805/OPCW-a-tool-in-hands-of-the-west-Douma-report

USA-UN-OPCW and Bustani

In 2002, the US government succeeded in having Brazilian diplomat José Maurício de Figueiredo Bustani[11] removed from the OPCW director-generalship. The issue was "how to address Iraq's *alleged* weapons of mass destruction."

In 2019 (October), Bustani was part of a Courage Foundation hearing in which an OPCW whistleblower gave evidence related to "the Douma chemical attack." Bustani later wrote that "'the convincing evidence of

---

[11] Brazilian diplomat José Maurício de Figueiredo Bustani was the Organization for the Prohibition of Chemical Weapons' first director-general. He held a law degree from Pontifical Catholic University of Rio de Janeiro and was a graduate of the Rio Branco Institute (Portuguese: Instituto Rio Branco; Abbreviation: IRBr), a graduate school of International Relations and diplomatic academy whose completion is an absolute prerequisite for entry into diplomatic service in Brazil. (It should be noted that US ambassadors are appointees who are not required to have studied in the field of international relations or diplomacy or to meet any pertinent academic or experiential prerequisites or standards.) During his career, Bustani was Brazil's ambassador in several countries: the United Kingdom between 2003 and 2008, and France from 2008 until his retirement in 2015. "Bustani," Wikipedia Foundation, updated May 7, 2022, https://en.wikipedia.org/wiki/Jos%C3%A9_Bustani "Rio Branco Institute," Wikipedia Foundation, updated August 6, 2021, https://en.wikipedia.org/wiki/Rio_Branco_Institute "Instituto Rio Branco," official website in Portuguese, http://www.institutoriobranco.itamaraty.gov.br/

irregular behavior in the OPCW investigation of the *alleged* Douma chemical attack confirms doubts and suspicions (he) already had.'"

In 2020 (October), Bustani was scheduled to testify at the United Nations Security Council (the body comprised of five inordinately powerful unelected entities (USA, UK, France, Russia, China) holding sole permanent membership) about the *alleged* cover up by the OPCW regarding the Douma chemical attack. (Again.) "The United States, Britain and France blocked Bustani from testifying (silenced a highly accomplished diplomat)—based on the twisted logic of a prior event they had caused, i.e., the departure of Bustani from the OPCW, was cause for preventing his testifying before the Council).

Death of a Nation

Robinson, Paul. "Biden's Russia policy ludicrous, unbelievable, contradictory & unprecedented: First offers Putin summit & then imposes sanctions." April 15, 2021. https://www.rt.com/russia/521101-biden-putin-policy- RT news.rethink/

> Paul Robinson is a professor at the University of Ottawa who writes about Russian and Soviet history, military history, and military ethics. He is also author of the *Irrussianality* blog

"'Painful to watch': Joe Biden apparently gets lost at G7 summit, wanders into café." RT news. June 13, 2021. https://www.rt.com/usa/526465-biden-lost-cognitive-decline/

"'He's clearly suffering from dementia': Conservatives jeer as Biden mistakes Syria for Libya ahead of talks with Putin." RT news. June 13, 2021. https://www.rt.com/usa/526480-biden-dementia-syria-libya/

> *Not a laughing matter*: almost fifty years entrenched in Washington, a US gerontocratic head of state in public

statements confuses "Syria with Libya;"and is observed "wandering around a (European) cafe terrace, looking lost."

Carnelos, Marco. "The Great Game in central Asia is over - and America lost." *Middle East Eye:* Campaign against Sanctions and Military Intervention in Iran. August 27, 2021 http://campaigniran.com/casmii http://campaigniran.com/casmii/?q=node/14906

> The tragic epilogue in Afghanistan came as no surprise
> to those few analysts who knew the real dynamics of the
> conflict but were often ignored, or ridiculed.

"The United States has no permanent friends or enemies, only interests." Press TV news. June 16, 2021. https://www.presstv.com/ Detail/2021/06/16/660179/US-Human-Rights-abuser-preaches-Human-Rights-

> The United States continues to hurl accusations of
> human rights abuses, cyber attacks and other criminal
> activity at Russia, China, and several other players in
> the Global South.

"United States follows Soviet Union's path — Putin: 'The problem of empires is that they think they are so powerful that they can afford small inaccuracies and mistakes.'" TASS June 4, 2021. https://tass.com/ world/1299269

Hedges, Chris. "The US Collective Suicide Machine." *Consortium News.* July 27, 2021. https://consortiumnews.com/2021/07/27/chris-hedges-the-us-collective-suicide-machine/ July 27, 2021

> Like any empire in terminal decay, no one will be held
> accountable for the debacle (in Afghanistan) or for the
> other debacles in Iraq, Syria, Libya, Somalia, Yemen or
> anywhere else. Not the generals. Not the politicians. Not

the CIA and intelligence agencies. Not the diplomats. Not the obsequious courtiers in the press who serve as cheerleaders for war. Not the compliant academics and area specialists. Not the defense industry.

Human tragedy — at least 801,000 people have been killed by direct war (US aggression) in Iraq, Afghanistan, Syria, Yemen, and Pakistan; thirty-seven million people have been displaced in and from Afghanistan, Iraq, Pakistan, Yemen, Somalia, the Philippines, Libya, and Syria (Watson Institute Cost of War Project) — is reduced to a neglected footnote.

Years later, the American empire, copying its past practice, will "find itself desperately trying to destroy its own creation."

Rasmus, Jack. "What Happens January 6th, 20th & After? America's Declining Democracy." Kyklos Productions January 4, 2021. http://www.kyklosproductions.com/posts/index.php?p=438

Attempts to Check and Correct

"UN Security Council must Slam Killers of Yemeni people, not exalt them (says) Top Yemeni official" "For six years, this barbarous consortium and its partners have waged a 'devastating war' against a sovereign nation and its people. Press TV news. April 15, 2021. https://www.presstv.com/Detail/2021/04/15/649542/UN-Security-Council-must-slam-killers-of-Yemeni-people-than-to-exalt-them-Top-Yemeni-official

Press TV news April 15, 2021 "UN Security Council must slam killers of Yemeni people, not exalt them (says) Top Yemeni official" https://www.presstv.com/Detail/2021/04/15/649542/

UN-Security-Council-must-slam-killers-of-Yemeni-people-than-to-exalt-them-Top-Yemeni-official

The United Nations[12],[13] is composed of 193 member states as of 2022). The inordinately powerful United States-headquartered United Nations Security Council[14],[15],[16] is composed of five permanent members: the People's Republic of China, the French Republic, the Russian Federation, the United Kingdom of Great Britain and Northern Ireland, and the United States of America. Calls for reform to this World War II era relic have centered on

(a) Membership
(b) Veto held exclusively by five (China-France-Russia-UK-USA) permanent members
(c) Regional representation
(d) Size of an enlarged UNSC (the current UNSC has ten nonpermanent members)
(e) Working methods
(f) UNSC relationship with the UN General Assembly

"World must hold US to account for supporting Daesh, new terrorism: President Raeisi." Press TV news September 5, 2021. https://www.presstv.ir/Detail/2021/09/05/665904/

[12] United Nations, https://www.un.org/en

[13] "About Us," United Nations, https://www.un.org/en/about-us

[14] "General Assembly Adopts Landmark Resolution Aimed at Holding Five Permanent Security Council Members Accountable for Use of Veto: Amid growing criticism of inaction by the Security Council on the war in Ukraine, the General Assembly adopted a landmark resolution today aimed at holding the five permanent Council members accountable for their use of veto," 76th Session, 69th and 70th Meetings United Nations General Assembly Plenary Meetings Coverage GA/12417 April 26, 2022, https://www.un.org/press/en/2022/ga12417.doc.htm

[15] "Reform of the United Nations Security Council," Wikipedia Foundation, updated June 19, 2022, https://en.wikipedia.org/wiki/Reform_of_the_United_Nations_Security_Council

[16] "United Nations Security Council," Wikipedia Foundation, updated June 24, 2022, https://en.wikipedia.org/wiki/United_Nations_Security_Council

Raeisi-Macron-Iran-Afghanistan-Lebanon-US-Daesh-JCPOA-terrorism

Senate Bill S.2391 (117th Congress, 2021-2022: "National Security Powers Act" July 20, 2021https://www.congress.gov/bill/117th-congress/senate-bill/2391/text

A bill to provide for clarification and limitations with respect to the exercise of national security powers, and for other purposes

The National Security Powers Act Safeguards Congressional Prerogative in Use of Military Force, Emergency Powers, and Arms Exports by Cutting off Funding for Activities Lacking Authorization

2

Extremism: Infantilism, Kleptocracy

I N THE CONTEMPORARY era reaching back at least to Reagan's Washington, American leaders (of questionable character and caliber) have bonded with an incestuous breed revolving in and out of the US government. They have bonded with paymasters in major corporations who together off- shored and off-loaded (disestablished and ruined) US-created, owned and operated industry and enterprise including essential research, health and education, local farming and development. Instead of governing, public officials pandered. They concentrated enterprise instead of promoting free enterprise and diverse innovation. They decimated essential regulatory processes. When the inevitably dire consequences of their actions hit home and were painfully felt by all Americans, the incestuous and invested culprits in and around US leadership did not chant "me too." They chanted "not me."

They blamed and shamed American "deplorables," "coloreds," *others*; and *foreigners*. They manufactured demons, adversaries, bogeymen. They put on a long-running, 24/7 pageantry, a show, an all-out media circus whose sole role was (and is) to distract, to create and fuel fear and conflict, distrust, ignorance and division within and among Americans; between Americans and the world's peoples, leaders and entities; and between Americans and established post-World War II international bodies.

One example from the sphere of domestic blame is a piece of manipulative drivel that seeps through radio rants emanating from opposite ends of the ignorance meter. When not blaming China, Russia, Korea, Latin America and their leaders, these radio ranters blame one of two past US presidents for the dire conditions in the United States: James Earl "Jimmy" Carter Jr. (1977-1981) or Donald John Trump (2016-2020). It is true that neither of these presidents was perfect. No man is perfect. No nation of men (men in the universal sense) is perfect.

One was Southern—a trait commonly disparaged by the entrenched but appreciated by the masses; the Southerner is less likely to hide who he is and where he stands. Jimmy Carter traces his lineage back four centuries to the American South. Donald John Trump is not a US Southerner but he is not entirely a northern North American. His grandparents were Friedrich Trump and Elisabeth Christ Trump of Kallstadt, Kingdom of Bavaria, German Empire (southern Germany). It is hard to account for Donald Trump's bluntness, but being so makes him far less sinister than the entrenched, incestuous Potomac River insiders.

Both Carter and Trump took office at a time (in contemporary times) when Americans were in great turmoil (individually and collectively, morally and economically). Perhaps voters hoped these individuals' outside-the-Washington Beltway pedigree, their difference, would turn the tide.

Both were business men. One had public service experience; one had none. One was a devout Sunday teacher and devoted husband; one was a showman, rather lax in personal affairs and loose in public displays. In the American system, any man (or woman) of a certain age and origin is eligible to contend for the US presidency; and, clearly, there is a flaw in this process; but that discussion is for another time and place. The point is that both of these men were eligible at the time and they accepted the challenge when Americans were hurting and hungering for decisive change.

However, the contemporary crop of leaders and their partners—having never relinquished power—wrested control and resumed the status quo.

They carried on: instead of sensing the pain of the nation and setting about solving serious problems facing the nation, these incestuous leaders and partners, with their every move, have compounded and deepened the breach. Not once over the past forty years has a US president set a permanent schedule for meeting with governors of the fifty states; instead, they have played one state against another and one governor against another. When their methods have failed or their targets refuse to heel, they punish. In foreign affairs, they ratchet up the aggression — dispatch banner headlines bleeding propaganda. They plant venal operatives, deploy bombs, tanks, hovering helicopters, robotic missiles, and sinister technology made to order by their nonprofit, think tank, multinational (cartel-like) partners and paymasters.

This pattern of incest, neglect, divisiveness, and aggression—this anti-American annihilative extremism—has left the nation and its people weakened and wanting. Languishing in a perpetual state of *unpreparedness*.

The *betrayal* continues. US officials' legalization of extortion manifest in the federal funding and enriching of nonprofit profiteers, including religious "charities" has turned ordinary Americans into beggars for what is or should be their rights under law. In the words of the Constitution of the United States, citizens have the right to expect their government to provide for and promote the *common* defense and *general* welfare of all Americans. Basic rights are further inscribed in the 1948 Universal Declaration of Human Rights.

Yet, Americans are made to beg and are held in contempt by tax-exempt groups that are designed not to solve problems or improve situations (*provide for the common defense and promote the general welfare*) but to perpetuate dependency. If American veterans suffering the horrors of repeated deployments to Washington's permanent theaters of aggression refuse the handouts of nonprofit profiteers and go directly to the streets to beg, a "public service" radio voice reeking of contempt announces that beggars should not be given money "because they are not homeless."

I remember a literacy nonprofit "executive director" who used to sit in her nine-ish-to-five-ish office playing with her dog and presiding over donated materials she denied to people needing them; and closed the doors to volunteer teachers who needed the materials to teach people seeking to improve their reading literacy. Obviously, the illiterate remained illiterate, and dependent.

The present era is unlike earlier periods. In the Depression era of Franklin Roosevelt's New Deal, people received useful training, earned wages doing useful work that needed to be done, created and otherwise produced what needed to be produced or created. Through the work, the people developed independence, and a sense of self worth and confidence.

In the contemporary era, there is a nonprofit profiteering machinery of corrupt, self-serving individuals acting as controller and manipulator of the masses. The machinery walls off the people from government of by and for the people. Unchecked and unmonitored executive directors are free to sit in their offices and play with their pets. Writing clever proposals and "mission" statements keep them in operation, at least until the soft money runs out. But improving literacy or anything else is neither the aim nor the end of the nonprofit profiteering industry. Nonprofits are a sham, a portrait in wastefulness pandered to and promoted by politicians and public officials in search of kickbacks of one kind or another. The contemporary crop of public officials, nonprofits, and shell foundations are *of a kind*. They create nothing and improve nothing. They instill dependency and contribute to societal regress. They enrich themselves, a narrow segment of society, at the expense of the United States of America and its people.

This character of *legalized* corruption is pervasive and corrosive. It underlies the chronic state of America's unpreparedness. Loose talk about "socialism" and "communism" and "liberalism" and "conservatism," the "neo-" of these, and a vast array of splitting "isms" of one tribe or another are vacuous distractions comprising a deadly form of extremism that denies genuine, time-honored rights of the citizenry. It creates interminable sickness, breakdown, and relentless unpreparedness.

The character of government officials matches the character of men and women who operate the nonprofit profiteering industry. Contemporary government of *by* and *for* the people is made up of individuals whose motive on entering government is to take on the trappings of status that inhere to position and hang on for life, and by any means necessary. Their primary purpose is *personal gain at the expense of the governed.* This kleptocracy and infantilism, a character of depraved selfishness and corruption incarnate—accompanied by a round-the-clock show distracting from its motive—sets and cements constant *conflict* and *unpreparedness* in America.

UNPREPAREDNESS

Infantilism seeks to deceive and distract. It is a state of arrested development (stunted growth or decline) in adult life: a pattern of expression manifesting childish mental or emotional qualities. In the present context, infantilism—deadly in public figures, politicians, government officials, and other influencers—is viewed as a form of extremism evident in tantrums (*violence in all things*). Failing to act with self-discipline, honor, and courage; excusing self, denying responsibility, and casting blame on other people, places, or things; preferring pageantry and manipulative language (insult, threat, obfuscation, and fabrication); and perversion of reality.

Infantilism in men and women (left, right, or color coded) operates in a parallel sphere, without regard for country, society, or social contract. Moral principles, law, and order are confined to lesser mortals (perhaps to Hillary Clinton's "deplorables").

Government officials' message to Americans at least over the past forty years has been "You're on your own." A B-movie actor decries the institution of government; a slick "Willie" disgraces it. Bodies pile up on the streets, in tunnels, and under bridges. In defiance of the 1948 Universal Declaration of Human Rights institutionalizing the right to shelter, American Ivy Leaguers declare shelterlessness a universal "right"; and one of their members, a "Yalie," declares the homeless *deplorables* and the assassination of a national leader *laughable*.

Education is fundamental to all advancement—even more so in a globalized world. Government must assist the general public as a matter of "common" and national defense, not as a matter of convenience (like US officials' convenient enemies and allies in foreign affairs), pandering to, manipulating, giving to or taking from this or that faction as another election cycle approaches. Government officials must strengthen America by strengthening its people: top-prioritizing, providing for, and ensuring quality education, training, retraining, apprenticeship; envisioning and planning work and workplaces; providing transitioning measures; and ensuring stable labor forces for the future, labor forces in which workers earn decent, livable wages.

Government officials must strengthen America by ensuring healthy individuals and healthy communities. Promoting drugs and varieties of addictive procedures, instruments, and substances—in the give-and-take of government officials and corporations—constitutes corruption. It is obviously harmful to individuals and communities.

The deaths and illnesses of millions in the pandemic of 2019 are the latest and perhaps the most glaring illustration of US officials' incompetence and corruption. Years of failure to carry on clean (objective) and continuous government investigative research, monitoring, regulating, and reporting was on display for everyone to see. Failure to ensure clean, incorruptible, and diligent institutions of health and centers for disease prevention was undeniable. The CDC (Centers for Disease Control and Prevention) became interchangeable with corporate liquid sugar factories and corporate drug factories. US personnel partnered with and swung back and forth between government and factories of harm.

It was patently clear that government officials no longer took their duty seriously: the duty of government to investigate, monitor, regulate, and report objective findings to and for the public good. Public officials had engaged in a pattern of promoting conflict and aggression in foreign lands instead of promoting the common defense and general welfare of America and its people. Officials' crime of corruption, with the gleeful aid of major media, was covered up by a constant screed of blame. America suffered and continues to suffer across essential sectors of health, education, and welfare.

Teacher Shortage, Lowered Standards

In the United States, long before the pandemic of 2019 and all the false moves made by US leaders in that regard, there has been a critical shortage of teachers and qualified teachers for America's classrooms. An Economic Policy Institute study has found that published estimates of America's increasing teacher shortage (for various reasons such as salary, classroom conditions, certification, retirements, resignations) have understated "the further magnitude of the problem," in that these estimates fail to show the unevenness in the shortage of qualified teachers. The worst deficit is being experienced by the United States' "high-poverty schools."[17]

The severe teacher shortage is long-term and long-neglected, multifaceted, interconnected, and has far-reaching societal and economic consequences. Some schools struggle to find and retain highly qualified individuals for their classrooms. Some school administrators allow vacancies to persist. Some of the factors that have been found

[17] Emma García and Elaine Weiss, "The teacher shortage is real, large and growing, and worse than we thought: The first report in 'The Perfect Storm in the Teacher Labor Market' series," Economic Policy Institute March 26, 2019, https://www.epi.org/publication/the-teacher-shortage-is-real-large-and-growing-and-worse-than-we-thought-the-first-report-in-the-perfect-storm-in-the-teacher-labor-market-series/ https://www.epi.org/research/teacher-shortages/

to hamper the achievement of quality basic education and effective teaching and learning are as follows:

- outside sources' interference with curricula
- school budgeting priorities and use of resources
- school boards and administrations unfitness for purpose
- comparatively low salaries against high costs of living, housing
- inappropriate class sizes
- insufficient professional, collegial, administrative, or complementary staff support
- insufficient time for professional development or in-service training
- school environments that may be characterized by lax or insufficient school community and pupil discipline (police officers deployed in schools means that school discipline has long since failed), and consequent feelings of fear and physical safety insecurity
- student (family) impoverishment
- language, multilingual or multi-cultural barriers, without sufficient multilingual professionals
- insufficient proper parent-teacher-school interaction

In the United States' kindergarten through twelfth grade (K-12) classrooms, more than 31 percent of the people allowed to teach in these classrooms lacked education in the subject matter field to which they were assigned. More than 22 percent lacked essential years of teaching experience. Almost 20 percent were allowed to teach without having successfully completed the traditional teacher certification process.

In "low-poverty" schools, 27.5 percent of teachers lack educational background (study, credentialing) in the subject area to which they are assigned. In "high-poverty" schools, 33.8 percent of teachers lack educational background (study, credentialing) in the subject area to which they are assigned. Low-poverty schools lacking full certification comprised 7.1 percent, and high-poverty schools in the same category comprised 9.9 percent. In schools employing teachers without the essential teaching experience, 19.8 percent were in low-poverty schools and 24.6 percent were in high-poverty schools. The percentages of people teaching in US schools who entered through a "nontraditional" or "alternative" route were 13.3 percent in low-poverty schools and 18.9 percent in high poverty schools.

Low-poverty schools are described as schools in which a teacher's assigned student group comprises "less than 25 percent" eligibility for "free or reduced-price lunch programs"; and high-poverty schools are those in which a teacher's assigned student group comprises "50 percent or more" eligibility for "free or reduced-price lunch programs."

The Economic Policy Institute's research together with published standards of the US Department of Education suggests the following essential teaching credentials.

- Full certification "with a regular, standard state certificate or advanced professional certificate" (not mere partial completion of these steps)
- Completion of the "traditional route" into teaching, meaning participation in a traditional certification program (not an "alternative certification program," i.e., a program such as "'a state, district, or university alternative certification program'" that was designed "'to expedite the transition of non-teachers to a teaching career'")
- Completion of more than five years of teaching experience
- Completion of knowledge background in subject matter of main assignment, i.e., bachelor or master's degree in the main teaching assignment field: an academic degree in relevant "general education," "special education," or "subject-matter specific" teaching assignment (not absence of educational background in the subject of main assignment).[18]

---

[18] The website All Education Schools, self- described as "a comprehensive online directory of accredited teacher education programs and teaching career resources,"

Government should lead by setting high standards, instead of modeling poor examples. Tolerance of low-caliber personnel among government officials, lowered or nonexistent standards or pertinent qualifications among media and government personnel is a tolerance that seems transmissible to or is replicated in US institutions of learning. As Washington models substandard behavior, all society reaps the consequences. As public office deteriorates, society is weakened. Contrary to conventional wisdom, it is not the office (or "the government") that is the culprit. It is the caliber and character of individuals who populate public office together with distracted, polarized, lazy, indifferent, deliberately ignorant media personalities and citizens at large who are complicit in the breakdown.

Critical areas of consideration that should precede employment, nomination or appointment are documented and demonstrated mental and psychological conditions, pertinent (directly related to a public office or department) experiential training and educational credentials, personal and professional character, demeanor, ethical record, command of the English language and skills and abilities in written and oral communication, as well as skills in and propensity for rational debate and civil intercommunication.

The argument that early settlers or early American leaders and drafters of major documents were often not credentialed or lacked higher education is a specious one because the level of general literacy in earlier times

---

lists the traditional route to teacher certification as: completion of an undergraduate degree (4-year program) plus a teacher preparation program; completion of a graduate (5th year) degree in an area of specialization; completion of an individual state's teaching requirements ((state requirements vary); pass standardized teaching examination (as required by a state); file application for and obtain state teacher certification

https://www.alleducationschools.com/teacher-certification/#:~:text=All%20 states%20require%20certified%20teachers%20to%20hold%20a,certain%20 subject%20matter%20or%20a%20specific%20grade%20level.

All Education Schools, All Star Directories, Inc, https://www.alleducationschools. com/about/

was far greater (morals far less lax) than the level of general literacy in the homes of Americans in contemporary times. Moreover, the level of literacy and ethical behavior has decreased drastically, carelessly over time. The growth of "home schooling" and "charter schooling" (the latter often a mere moneymaking scheme like so much nonprofit profiteering, the former a 24/7 recess)—together with fickle federal grant-making and a lack of essential uniformity across states— has resulted in disastrous consequences for American pupils and their access to strong comprehensive education that includes emphasis on self-discipline, civics, and practice in interacting congenially and civilly with society at large.

If plumbers and electricians are required to meet qualifying standards for their work, why should teachers and government officials—having power over millions of people and over death-dealing weaponry, and over young and impressionable minds—be exempt from qualifying standards? They should not be exempt. People permitted to hold public office should be required to meet and maintain high qualifying standards; and people permitted to hold school positions (on boards, administrative staffs, teaching faculties) should be required to meet established and enforced qualifying standards and certifications.

Health Sector Shortage

As with education, so it is with health. The United States is unprepared in the areas of medicine and health.

Before the 2019 pandemic, there was the 1980s acquired immunodeficiency syndrome (AIDS) epidemic. As the AIDS crisis spread across the nation in the 1990s (amid widespread, loudly broadcast prejudice and attempts to cast blame on afflicted Americans and on other countries), Americans found themselves without enough homegrown "healers." Foreigners whose native tongues and cultures were incomprehensible to Americans became the *saviors*, the *common defense* of available health professionals that America's leadership had failed to fund, to educate, to promote and provide.

In the state of Nevada, as of 2021, "nearly a quarter of physicians" were reportedly *new* immigrants. Thirty-seven percent of nurses are immigrant. The general attitude of US officials toward and treatment of these professionals is not unlike US officials' treatment of interpreters and translators on site in foreign countries. Foreign-born health professionals are mere conveniences to be used, abused, and discarded.

Jessica Kutz writes at *High Country News*, "Whenever labor is seen as an exportable commodity—something you can turn on and off with barely a moment's notice—exploitation tends to follow." The story is that foreign medical workers have been held in limbo or threatened by visa or residency requirements, which often fluctuate, whimsically, from one US administration to another. Employers sometimes threaten immigrant physicians with deportation if they do not obey employer demands—demands to accept intolerably long hours of work (harmful to worker and patients) and demands to keep silent about an employer's breach of contract concerning salary.

The pandemic of 2019 (and years following) has caused medical institutions and services to be severely curtailed or eliminated. Critical medical staffs have been laid off. Projections by *High Country News* public health journal reported in 2021 that by 2030, the states of New Mexico, Nevada, Montana, Idaho, and Arizona "will suffer some of the worst physician shortages in the country." Thirty-seven percent of physicians in the state of New Mexico will retire in the decade that extends from 2021 to 2031.

The concern of America's leaders is not heath but private wealth and masking problems. Political campaigns and elected officials have been kept in office by drug companies. In the 2019–2020 listing by OpenSecrets (Center for Responsive Politics) of the top five pharmaceuticals and health products company contributors to politicians was as follows:

DE Shaw Research (molecular manipulation tech)	$5,989,834
Pulse Biosciences (cosmetic / medical tech)	$4,647,012
Pfizer Inc (pharma / biotech)	$3,091,640
Masimo Corp (medical tech)	$2,699,727
Alexion Pharmaceuticals (AstraZeneca subsidiary)	$2,489,103

OpenSecrets listing of the top five takers of drug money in 2021–2022 were:

Biden, Joseph	Presidential	$8,403,799
Trump, Donald	Presidential	$2,642,163
Sanders, Bernard VT	Senate	$1,301,069
Harrison, Jaime R SC	2020 Senate primary candidate	$904,557
Ossoff, Thomas Jonathan GA	Senate	$883,522

The top five drug and medical contributors in 2021–2022 were:

Starkey Hearing Technologies (global instruments)	$564,300
Masimo Corp (med tech)	$533,714
Pfizer Inc Pfizer Inc (drugs / biotech)	$497,004
RAAS Nutritionals LLC (drugs)	$400,100
Abbott Laboratories (drugs / medical devices)	$294,172

The top ten recipients of drug and medical industry funding reported in 2022 were as follows:

Drug/medical industry's top ten recipients of 2022:

#1	Charles E. Schumer NY	Senate	$222,433
#2	Cathy M. Rodgers WA	House	$146,160
#3	Scott Peters CA	House	$128,450
#4	Todd Young IN	Senate	$106,325

#5	Kyrsten Sinema AZ	Senate	$100,200
#6	Catherine C. Masto NV	Senate	$94,537
$7	Anna Eshoo CA	House	$89,950
#8	Tim Scott SC	Senate	$89,930
#9	Brett Guthrie KY	House	$82,750
#10	Patty Murray WA	Senate	$80,975

The total taken by all candidates was reported by OpenSecrets as $6,432,937. OpenSecrets reports were based on the latest data published in the Federal Election Commission reports. [19]

In the post-Cold War era, the crisis concerning prescription drugs in the United States was created and sustained by separate (but related in kind) industrial complexes joined at the hip of government officials (politicians, agencies, institutions): the military industrial complex's man-made Afghanistan crisis and the medical industrial complex's man-made opioid crisis.

According to the US Centers for Disease Control, between the end of the 1990s and 2012 the "amount of prescription opioids sold to pharmacies, hospitals, and doctors' offices nearly quadrupled." Those most affected by the opioid crisis were people living in what has been called the opioid belt: a geographical area stretching from Webster County, West Virginia, through southern Virginia and through Monroe County, Kentucky (more than ninety mostly rural counties experiencing the highest per capita opioid death rates). From 2006 through 2012, this opioid belt's death rates were "4.5 times the national average." Findings from the CDC and National Institutes of Health showed the following excesses between the years 2006 and 2020.

[19] "Pharmaceuticals / Health Products" Summary of "Top Contributors 2021-2022," "Top Recipients 2021-2022," OpenSecrets, updated with data released by the Federal Election Commission on May 23, 2022, https://www.opensecrets.org/industries/indus.php?ind=H04

- 2006–2014: Physicians dispensed "2.17 billion prescriptions" across the United States, each prescription capable of allowing "up to ninety pills."

- 2013: Health providers "wrote nearly 250 million opioid prescriptions."

- 2016–2017 in the US Midwest: "Opioid overdoses increased by 70 percent."

- 2017: Nearly "50,000" Americans died from opioid overdose; and "1.7 million people" in the United States suffered from "substance abuse disorders related to prescription opioid pain relievers."

In November 2021, in a big show of *something being done* about a crisis long out of control, Reuters reported that the pharmaceutical corporation Purdue (owned by the Sackler family) had entered a guilty plea to three criminal counts for violating a federal anti-kickback law, defrauding the United States, and violating the Food, Drug and Cosmetic Act. However, as this book is being written, the name of the Sackler family (Purdue opioid makers) still adorns New York's American Museum of Natural History (Sackler Educational Laboratory), Dia Art Foundation (Sackler Institute), and the Guggenheim Museum (Sackler Center for Arts Education).

The American Bar Association had reported in September 2019 that America's opioid crisis had ravaged urban, suburban, and rural communities in every state of the United States. According to its report at the time, citing other studies, "115 people die every day in the United States from opioid overdose" and "400,000" had died in a twenty-year period. In 2019, "more than 2 million people" were reported to have been "living with an opioid-related substance use disorder."

The projection in loss of life over the period between 2019 and 2029 was "650,000" people. Yet US government leaders' actions (together with those of state and local leaders and people in the medical field) have been generally superficial, ineffective, or contributive to the crisis.

Government officials and drug makers are wedded, unchecked, and in conflict with the common defense and general welfare. In a 2020 article, American physician Andrew Kolodny explained how the opioid crisis was twenty years in the making by men and women in government.

Over a twenty-year period, scores of Food and Drug Administration personnel, Kolodny reported, had been "involved in opioid approvals" who left the FDA and joined the staff of opioid makers. For example, "principal FDA reviewers who originally approved Purdue's oxycodone application (took) positions at Purdue after leaving the agency." In 2019 "the head of FDA's analgesic division retired from the FDA (with 'more than 30 years of experience') and started her own consulting business, which promises drug makers 'help' to 'successfully and efficiently bring your products to market.'"

Kolodny reported that FDA's "close ties to the (drug / pharmaceutical) industry" factored into its decision to rely on "a controversial methodology called enriched enrollment randomized withdrawal (EERW) … described by critics as '"cooking the books."'

The Food and Drug Administration more generally lacks adequate oversight. The agency "erred in permitting "promotion of opioid use for chronic pain," Dr. Kolodny wrote. Even while the crisis was in full tilt, FDA's "policies for approving and labeling opioids remained largely unchanged." Personnel have failed to undertake "a root-cause analysis of (FDA's) regulatory errors that contributed to (the opioid) public health catastrophe (or) to institute any major reforms."

The FDA response, Kolodny concluded, has been to blame. For more than twenty years, top officials at the Center for Drug Evaluation and

Research defended the "FDA's handling of opioids, claiming that the agency has properly enforced the Food, Drug, and Cosmetic Act." On paper, the Act mandates "adequate and well-controlled studies" as prerequisites to product approval and promotion "as safe and effective."[20]

A single characteristic of the kleptocrat and mercenary is a kind of Wild West anarchism that says: *For me and mine, anything goes* in the quest for money (wealth, power, riches). For these women and men (me and mine), whether graduates of Harvard's medical school or Erik Dean Prince's contract-killer school, everything is purchasable (marketable, fodder for investment)—death, even life itself. *Nothing's sacred among the godly.*

Thus, a cabal of venal, corrupt, mercenary, unethical government officials and drug makers and medical and health professionals and profiteering nonprofits and media conspired against the health and welfare of the people of the United States. Together with their shyster lawyers, statisticians, and consultants calculating profit and loss, how to get away with crime and cruelty, and how much, if caught, to *settle* (what judge, what court district, what little fish to sacrifice, what amount of assets to give up or appear to give up to silence clean reporting and hush cries for law, order, and justice) short of full-sweep prison sentences or admitting wrongdoing—the cabal of public-private partnering laid the groundwork for and looked away from *killer-pill mills.*

---

[20] Andrew Kolodny, MD, is executive director of Physicians for Responsible Opioid Prescribing and senior scientist and the medical director of the Opioid Policy Research Collaborative in the Heller School for Social Policy and Management at Brandeis University, Waltham, Massachusetts. Dr. Kolodny is instructor at the Columbia University Mailman School of Public Health regarding the opioid crisis. His article "How FDA Failures Contributed to the Opioid Crisis" appeared in the August 2020 edition of the American Medical Association Journal of Ethics.

Freedom, Capitalism Run Amok
Profiteering Pill Mills and Physicians

Pill-mill physicians have been called drug dealers in white coats. They are physicians who amassed fortunes "by putting millions of opioid pills on the street." Their *work* is said to follow a deadly pattern: They demand "hundreds of dollars in cash" for an initial client visit lasting a few minutes. They then charge "more money for refill visits" lasting fewer minutes than the initial visit. Undercover officers are said to have testified at trial that such visits have lasted under two minutes, and the pill mill doctors have permitted *victims, prospective patients* to select their own drug of choice. "Surveillance and paper records" have provided evidence of "doctors seeing up to 100 patients a day, but conducting little or no physical examinations or diagnostic tests." A doctor's "fake patients" would even carry opioid-prescribed drugs, "unnecessary prescriptions," to pharmacies where they were filled, without question; then sold on the streets. A cut of the profits from street sales was then kicked back to the physician, or *healthcare* provider. And the white collars escape virtually unscathed.

When the culprits are caught and charged in federal court, when the evidence is overwhelming, Adam Gershowitz wrote in a study focused on inconsistent sentencing, the length of a sentence often depends on "the age of the perpetrator."[21], [22], [23]

---

[21] Adam M. Gershowitz, "The Opioid Doctors: Is Losing your License a Sufficient Penalty for Dealing Drugs?" Hastings Law Journal 72, 871 (2019), (Last revised November 6, 2021), SSRN, https://ssrn.com/abstract=3566600 https://papers.ssrn.com/sol3/papers.cfm?abstract_id=3566600

[22] Adam M. Gershowitz, "Punishing Pill Mill Doctors: Sentencing Disparities in the Opioid Epidemic," UC Davis Law Review 54, 1053 (December 13, 2019), SSRN (Last revised November 5, 2021), https://papers.ssrn.com/sol3/papers.cfm?abstract_id=3503662 https://ssrn.com/abstract=3503662 or http://dx.doi.org/10.2139/ssrn.3503662

[23] Adam M. Gershowitz at William & Mary Law School is R. Hugh and Nolie Haynes Professor of Law specializing in criminal law, criminal law (white collar

Life Imitates Art Imitating Life. In Agatha Christie's 1932 story *Peril at End House,* later adapted for screen, Ms. Lemon has a scene in which she reports her findings of a visit to London's medical row at Holly Street. She tells Hercule Poirot (the star detective) that the physician uncle of one of the main characters is a "woman's" doctor (*woman* meaning "neurotic," she explains) with high-class clients whom he sees for *only a few moments.* The nephew, the Royal Navy "commander" owner-operator of a private ship (character), visits the doctor every ten days. It turns out that the nephew, dressed in navy blues, is a cocaine drug trafficker and his Holly Street physician uncle is a drug dealer. Yesterday's fictional Holly Street is today's factual Pill Mill.

America under Water

From health emergencies or routine health and medical services to great weather events, the prevailing negligence causes and compounds crises. Governance is not governance but, rather, hit-and-miss patchwork in the middle of yet another crisis.

In September 2021, Daniel de Vries commented on Hurricane Ida and Americans' failure to heed the decades-long warnings of scientists concerning the consequences of global climate change and the United States' "abysmal lack of preparedness." Referencing the 2019 US National Climate Assessment report, de Vries wrote that much of the infrastructure in the Northeastern United States (including drainage and sewer systems, flood and storm protection assets, transportation systems, and power supply) "is nearing the end of its *planned* life expectancy," and is unprepared to sustain the "projected wider variability of future climate conditions."

The big storms of the twenty-first century have included the following:

---

crime), and criminal procedure law, https://law2.wm.edu/faculty/bios/fulltime/amgershowitz.php

- Hurricane Katrina in 2005 that left 1,836 people dead and caused massive loss in Louisiana (especially Greater New Orleans). Flood-control systems designed years earlier by the US Army Corps of Engineers had failed. The Corps claimed immunity from liability under federal statute. Damages were estimated at $125 billion. Other affected regions and states included Alabama, Bahamas, Canada (mostly eastern), Cuba, Florida (South, Central, Panhandle), and Mississippi.

- Hurricane Sandy in 2012 was reportedly the deadliest, most destructive, and strongest hurricane of the 2012 Atlantic hurricane season. It left 233 people dead and caused an estimated $68.7 billion in damages. Other affected areas included Bahamas, Bermuda, Canada (mostly eastern), Greater Antilles (Caribbean Sea islands of Cuba, Hispaniola, Puerto Rico, Jamaica, and Cayman), and United States (especially the coastal Mid-Atlantic States).

- Hurricane Ida in 2021 was recorded as the second most damaging and intense hurricane after Hurricane Katrina that recorded landfall in Louisiana. It left 115 people dead and caused an estimated $75.25 billion in damages. Other areas affected included Cayman Islands, Colombia, Cuba, Jamaica, United States Gulf (mostly Louisiana) and east (mostly the northeastern) coasts, and Venezuela.

In his commentary, Daniel de Vries observed that when Hurricane Ida came to New York, damage to the transit system caused by Sandy was still in disrepair. "Much of the shoreline remained dangerously unprotected"; and instead of "mobilizing billions of dollars to provide adequate housing for the masses of workers," public officials "squandered immense city resources … on constructing luxury homes in the clouds."

Thus in the midst the 2021 storm, de Vries said,

The entire public transportation network ground to a halt ..., not as a preparatory measure to protect the public; but out of necessity once the system ceased to be navigable. Subway lines functioned as sewers and waterfalls cascaded down onto subway platforms, stranding passengers for hours. Roadways across the region were transformed into raging rivers, submerging cars and motorists alike. Rainwater and sewage engulfed homes across several states.

New Jerseyans also suffered. De Vries recalled floodwaters around a housing complex in Elizabeth that killed four residents and left six hundred homeless. More than a dozen New Jersey inhabitants died in vehicles. Eleven people, trapped in flooded New York City basement apartments, died from drowning.

Louisiana and Mississippi had lost some 16 people at the time of his writing. The victims included "four nursing home residents," who had been evacuated two days before the hurricane struck and herded into "a filthy warehouse lacking facilities for the more than 800 residents." These people had died from injuries and from "electrocution and carbon monoxide poisoning."

Among American leaders is a casual carelessness regarding the health and welfare of the American public that, sadly, leaves one unsurprised at the deaths of millions in the pandemic headlined in 2019 and a succession of climate disasters visited upon crumbling structures and *governance by chaos* and deliberate incompetence funneling trillions— in de Vries's words— "into the markets to boost the fortunes of the financial oligarchy."

Sky's Falling

In all the waste, nothing is safe or sound. *The sky is falling*, too. The United States is purportedly home to the "finest military" machine makers in the world, but reality tells a different story.

What is true is this: US government officials, many of them riding the revolving door in and out of government, extort and waste America's trillions on corrupt, inept, unprepared men and machinery that presents an ever-present danger to America and other countries. The long and persisting story of Boeing is well documented. Added to this in recent years have been the spectacle (not talked about by Washington inmates and their major media) of falling (i.e., failing) US helicopters.

In September 2021, Military.com reported rising incidents of US manned aircraft crashes per 100,000.

- 2019: five severe incidents
- 2020: nine severe incidents
- 2021: eleven severe incidents

One naval aviator is reported to have admitted that "it takes moral courage" for his military colleagues "to admit" unpreparedness: "[that] we are not proficient in executing a training mission or an operational mission as it was designed."

Twelve marines died in a helicopter crash off the coast of Oahu, Hawaii. Five years later, "the Navy released a 'lessons learned' (American propaganda for what they never do in practice, "learn lessons") document on the incident." This latest report came on the heels of another investigation that had found marine leadership to be deficient, inept, and thus incapable of preventing training accidents and deaths.

Instead of recommending the proper training content, quality, and duration, the latest report instructs pilots, meaninglessly, "to be realistic" about their flight training and flying proficiency.

In July 2021, a report by the US Government Accountability Office showed that, over a ten-year period (2011-2021), "123 US soldiers and Marines" stationed inside the United States "had died in non-combat tactical vehicle accidents." The major reason for the incidents was US military services' failure to adequately carry out "their own safety measures."

Waste, greed, graft, neglect, calculated incompetence combined with deregulation and discontinuance of proper government oversight—legalized corruption, *capitalism run amok* extremism—and Flight USA (domestic and transcontinental) returns to an era preceding Wilbur and Orville Wright.

"Right" to Shelterlessness

Like their volunteerism scam, American extremists tell their fellow citizens that they have a "right" to live in tents and tunnels and under bridges; a "right" to subsist with no essential facilities, hygiene, or privacy; a "right" to line and litter public streets under the derisive contempt of onlookers.

For more than a decade (*at least forty years of neglect*), the United States has made no actual advancement "in reducing the number of Americans at risk of homelessness." The problems and the suffering have worsened instead of gotten better. In the area where I live, a woman's voice on the radio demonizes "panhandlers" as not really homeless people but "drug addicts" looking for money to feed their habit. (Drug addiction is an illness that needs the services of proper institutions of health.) The voice claims that the information she is spreading via the public airwaves is based on an "informal study."

However an organization that conducts legitimate and longer-term studies of homelessness in America (the National Alliance to End Homelessness) has found that, before the 2019 pandemic, there were 580,466 people languishing in homelessness. The data included these categories:

- Individuals: 408,891
- Families (people in): 171,575
- Chronically homeless (individuals): 110,528
- Homeless military veterans: 37,252
- Unaccompanied youth: 34,210

In America, the water is undrinkable. The streets are littered with debris. Thousands of people are homeless and without proper counseling and medical care. Uplift or advice helpful for transitioning into better conditions is inaccessible or unavailable.

Buses, trains, and planes (those that manage to stay in the air or on the rails) do not run on time. The transportation workforce is understaffed, inadequately trained, and ill-treated. Schools guarded by police officers are ill-equipped, crumbling, in decay, lacking necessary ventilation, learning materials, teachers, and proper discipline.

Native-born students with a fondness for hip-hop graffiti-splattered public spaces, a penchant for wielding lethal instruments against public statues and firearms against their teachers and fellow students seem to subsist on calculated ignorance and illiteracy, constant chaos. Too often they are untaught and incapable of self-discipline or the discipline of performing basic skills such as mathematical calculation and writing and speaking grammatically correct in the language of their homeland. Clever academics and commercial geniuses, nonprofit profiteers, pandering politicians and questionable intellectuals reinforce a condition of willful unpreparedness among the young. As they have promulgated the fallacious "right" of homelessness, the well-heeled have told America's young: "You have the 'right' to be undisciplined, illiterate, and unemployable"—Destination vagrancy, lawlessness, prison, or death.

BLAME INCREASES
PUBLIC TRUST DECREASES

American leadership and the upper crust has so thoroughly corrupted institutions of government, health, education, and welfare (including tearing down absolutely vital regulatory operations) that none can be trusted. No physician or psychiatrist or pharmacist, no teacher or administrator, no public official or voting precinct, no bridges or roadways, no mode of transportation can be trusted. Thanks to venal kleptocrats in high places (and professional nihilists bent on tearing down all traditions and intuitions) America's young and impressionable are exploited, ruthlessly, sacrificed to extremists' theaters of foreign and domestic aggression and to casual labor that, by definition (like death in war): teaches nothing and cares for no one; requires neither responsibility nor discipline; and goes nowhere, offers no future.

The same kleptocrats in high places would have America's millions of inhabitants believe (*what the world knows is untrue*) that the pain inflicted on America is caused by either the Chinese, the Russians, the Iranians, the Syrians, the Somalis, or any of those *other than "us."*

Anti-China *anti-American* Syndrome

Having failed to foresee or prepare for the 2019 epidemic, American leaders began a show of distraction that played one American (group, tribe, faction, state) against another. Leaders up and down the spectrum from Washington to the states took to the stage. They performed on television and ranted on social media platforms. Critical sectors of K-12 schooling were abandoned. Youngsters needed desperately to remain in classrooms, but they were dismissed, essentially, to fend for themselves.

In the midst of a multilayered widespread crisis, there was much that US leadership could have done for this Union but did not do.

They could have set their backs to the wheel, put on their best thinking caps. They could have gone beyond the Washington Beltway and found the best advice; initiated an on-the-ground all-out nationwide effort to benefit all US schools, no matter where they were located. Thousands of people could have been employed productively, doing vital work and earning living wages (instead being handed hush-do-nothing cash).

In schools, offices, and factories government leaders could have funded and ensured funding for air filtration systems and installation; on-the-spot renovations and continual upgrades; continuous manufacture and installation of hygiene dispensers and related disposal mechanisms; and supplying of protective gear for all inhabitants of buildings. Shoring up labor forces (with incentive pay and support) would have served to ensure constant operations and pertinent, substantive instruction and emotional support as needed, and continual remedial effort, equipment, supplies, and services.

Had public officials not chosen to pander to select groups, enrich millionaires, throw money to some of those fly-by-night foundations and nonprofits where stealing was predictable; had US leaders not chosen to stage a pageantry of playing one group against another and whipping up erroneous and otherwise distracting tales about other countries—huge numbers of Americans not only would have survived the pandemic of 2019 (and continuing), but they would have been strengthened in preparedness going into the future. The upper crust, their paymasters and sycophants did none of this in a full-out *We the People* effort. Instead, they created and recited slogans. They cast blame on US up states or down states, eastern or western states; and on the People's Republic of China.

In September 2021, members of the 117th Congress set out to prove *China's fault* for originating the virus. The US House Foreign Affairs

Committee put together a report claiming that the novel coronavirus escaped from the Wuhan Institute of Virology (WIV) "sometime prior to September 12, 2019"—at which time, their report claims, Chinese authorities brought in an army biological weapons expert and boosted security, ventilation, and air disinfection systems." (It's too bad the Americans, *We the People,* did not institute ventilation and air disinfection systems in US schools and workplaces.)

Also lockstep with his predecessor, President (former senator and vice presidential gerontocrat) Joseph Biden superintended a garbage-in/garbage-out, self-fulfilling prophecy project. Instead of focusing on ending the crisis, Biden ordered a "study" to keep the "China virus" anti-China syndrome going. This second unscientific exercise, having *not* ruled out "the possibility" of the 2019 virus originating in a Chinese laboratory, gave Washington red meat for continuing their "Beijing did it" exercise in distraction.

In the same pattern of US leaders' manufacturing erroneous facts and nonexistent phenomena, even after objective findings revealed the contrary (as in the pattern of "Iraqi weapons of mass destruction" and "Iranian nuclear weapons" and "Syrian chemical weapons" USA fabrications), US leaders were unalterable, fixed, in their promulgation of fiction. Despite the published results of an objective World Health Organization on-site four-week investigation that had been conducted by an assembly of experts (not spies) in China in early 2021, concluding that "the virus likely originated in an animal before spreading to humans in December 2019"—US leaders and media continued to press their distraction.

Chinese officials rightly rejoined that the US spy agencies' product was a "political manipulation" and "based on the presumption of guilt on the part of China." Moreover, the Washington move had served only to "disturb and sabotage international efforts on finding the source of the virus." The Washington distraction and characteristic failure to focus on and cooperate with other nations in solving a complex global problem—the same pattern repeated in domestic affairs among members of Congress, and between executive and legislative branches of government—the Chinese saw for what it was: a fabled distraction void of scientific foundation.

Moreover, in that many countries including the United States engage in laboratory research with micro viruses; and since the US use of viruses as weapons has been widely documented—any country could have been the site of origin of the germ. Any country could have been subjected to an investigation. Quite naturally, 4.7 million Chinese petitioned the World Health Organization to send experts to the United States' Fort Detrick bio lab military facility in Maryland, a move that was supported by the Chinese Foreign Ministry.

In the midst of crisis, the pressing challenge is not and should not be to compound the crisis, distract from it, or muddy the waters. Rational behavior would be to work diligently at home and with all nations to end the crisis. It would seem wise for nations to work together instead of engaging in a blame fest. China is right not to humor US officials' and media whims.

In the child, blaming others ("brother did it," "sister did it," "other classmates did it") is cute or part of early growth. Through good parenting, proper schooling, healthy growth and development, correction, honesty, self-responsibility will come as the child enters adulthood. In adults, blaming is a lethal act of cowardice. It breaks relationships, causes decay, and engenders crippling distrust. Americans' expressed antipathy for other nations and peoples manifests also a condition of weakness and self-loathing.

Victims of the American Brand

Who are the victims when Americans claim "humanitarianism?" For more than twenty years, just in the contemporary era, United States leaders have been bombing (ordering the bombing of) millions of people in the name of "humanitarianism" (killing is "good" for other countries and peoples). In early 2021, a Chinese official put it succinctly and painfully accurately: "The United States, rather than any other country, poses the *greatest threat to itself*" (emphasis added).

In the late 1990s, President Clinton took time off (or distraction from) his personal proclivity of bringing disgrace on the White House to command the obliteration of the Federal Republic of Yugoslavia. In contempt for and in defiance of the United Nations Security Council, and on the heels of an earlier NATO bombing of Bosnia and Herzegovina, the US president in 1999 authorized "the use of US Armed Forces in a NATO bombing campaign against Yugoslavia." Perhaps it is easier for a person who has failed to serve actively in a military capacity to order the slaughter of human beings. US presidents, in the contemporary era (circa 1961–2021), who have no record of active military service, include the men (women top officials are a whole other issue) listed below.

No service 1993–2001; 2009–2021

William Jefferson Clinton (born William Jefferson Blythe III)	42nd president 1993–2001
Barack Hussein Obama II	44th president 2009–2017
Donald John Trump	45th president 2017–2021
Joseph Robinette Biden Jr.	46th president 2021–

Reserve service 1961–1993; 2001

John Fitzgerald Kennedy (US Navy Res)	35th president 1961–1963
Lyndon Baines Johnson (US Navy Res)	36th president 1963–1969
Richard Milhous Nixon (US Navy Res)	37th president 1969–1974
Gerald Rudolph Ford Jr. (born Leslie Lynch King Jr.) (US Navy Res)	38th president 1974–1977
Ronald Wilson Reagan (US Army Res)	40th president 1981–1989
George Herbert Walker Bush (US Navy Res)	41st president 1989–1993

George Walker Bush (Air National Guard)	43rd president 2001–2009

The thirty-fourth and thirty-ninth US presidents, Dwight David Eisenhower (1953–1961) and James Earl Carter (1977–1981), respectively, served in the United States Army and the United States Navy. Excluded in the above context are reserves, which are standby units.[24]

As with all US violence in sovereign territories and interference in matters concerning other peoples and cultures, the human consequence is years of flooding refugees, most of whom are unwanted and openly disparaged by the very leadership positions that caused preexisting conditions forcing mass displacement of people from their homelands. The Clinton-era bombing of Yugoslavia caused mass displacement of Kosovo Serbs and other minorities. "A significant portion of Serbian Orthodox churches and Serbian cemeteries and homes" have been reported "demolished or vandalized." The pattern of contempt and reckless disregard for life associated with the US brand knows no bounds.

In a show of further contempt for the United Nations (and for human life), the 116th US Congress legislated a criminal US offensive against Syria and its leaders and unleashed debilitating sanctions against the Syrian economy, thus making life miserable for the country's civilians. Their 2019 piece of legislation called the Caesar Act was, in effect, a bill of brute force cloaked in "humanitarian" terms, i.e., the "Caesar Syria *Civilian Protection* Act" (emphasis added). The measure was concocted while Joseph Robinette Biden was holidaying between government stints, casually professing on the University of Pennsylvania faculty, and piling up multimillions in book deals and speaking fees. President Donald Trump signed Caesar in late 2019. It went into effect in June

---

[24] The National Guard reserve is a voluntary (US Army / Air Force) group that is available to state governors or a US president during a state emergency or national emergency. Such units reportedly are not even required to maintain "military skills" and "readiness."

of 2021. Violent humanitarianism does not discriminate among tribes: American partisans of all kinds maintain the brand.

On entering the US presidency, Joseph Biden ordered a lethal, unprovoked act of aggression against the Syrian Arab Republic. Bouthaina Shaaban[25] accurately described the display of extremism as "a complete manifestation of US unilateralism" in the face of (as with Clinton) obvious disapproval of the General Assembly of the United Nations. The UNGA is composed of 193 nations, not including associate members.

Wounds continuously wounded cannot heal, Columnist Will Bunch suggested. "I don't understand," Bunch wrote, "what gives Biden (or what gave his presidential predecessors Donald Trump, Barack Obama, and George W. Bush) the legal or moral authority to unilaterally launch a military attack in Syria, when there has been no declaration of war" (let alone provocation in the region or threat to the United States!). The only authorization of military force is "a 20-year old" reaction without due process of law "to events occurring on September 11, 2001." Bunch takes the sensible view that "some American traditions need to go away," among them "the insane yet deeply entrenched notion that a new US president 'earns his wings' (by dropping) some bombs on the Middle East or South Asia."[26]

---

[25] Bouthaina Shaaban is a former professor of romantic poetry at Damascus University, a Syrian politician and former First Minister of Expatriates for the Syrian Arab Republic (2002–2008), an adviser to the foreign ministry, and veteran interpreter for Syrian presidents Hafez al-Assad and Bashar al-Assad. She is well aware of Americans' acts and character of brute force. She is aware of the consequences and stands uncompromising on the matter of her country's sovereignty (as ordinary Americans would be about America), declaring that her country will always "resist US occupation, in all possible ways, until we reclaim all our occupied lands." Rings of early American Revolutionaries!

[26] Will Bunch is a columnist with the *Philadelphia Inquirer*. His opinion piece appeared on February 28, 2021.

In the spring of 2020, the International Committee of the National Lawyers Guild raised the alarm about the unilateral aggression of the United States and US officials' attempts to drive other nations into the dark ages:

- causing the rise and spread of illness, diseases, and starvation;
- causing a wedge among and between nations;
- stymieing nations' development; and
- undermining nations' sovereignty and the leadership of countries chosen by their citizenry.

The Guild's letter to US public officials pointed out that the "unilateral coercive measures" (UCMs) taken against Iran and Venezuela and secondary pressures taken against third-world countries stood in breach of the charters of the United Nations and the Organization of American States (OAS), both having been agreed to and both incorporated in US domestic law through Article 6 of the US Constitution. They noted that sanctions against Cuba, Venezuela, Iran, Syria, and Zimbabwe were in violation of international law; and that all US actions in this regard showed a flagrant disregard for the seventy-year-old set of principles and promises (coauthored by American diplomat Eleanor Roosevelt) agreed to and enshrined in the Universal Declaration of Human Rights.[27] The letter writers made particular note of Articles 3 and 25 of the Declaration: the right of every person "to life and a standard of living that is adequate for the health and well-being of individuals and their families, including food, clothing, housing, medical care and necessary social services."

---

[27] Universal Declaration of Human Rights proclaimed by the United Nations General Assembly in Paris, December 10, 1948 (General Assembly resolution 217 A) Article 3 "Everyone has the right to life, liberty and security of person." Article 25/1 "Everyone has the right to a standard of living adequate for the health and well-being of himself and of his family, including food, clothing, housing and medical care and necessary social services, and the right to security in the event of unemployment, sickness, disability, widowhood, old age or other lack of livelihood in circumstances beyond his control." https://www.un.org/en/about-us/universal-declaration-of-human-rights

DR. CAROLYN LADELLE BENNETT

The insidiously lowered caliber of the US diplomatic corps, the general lapse in professional standards ensures US global lawlessness including rejection of the jurisdiction of the International Court of Criminal Justice, and even the issuance of threats against ICC prosecutors. Matters are made worse as organizations such as Amnesty International and Human Rights Watch accept, explain away, or ignore American lawlessness.

In 2021, as United States leaders, American media, and various American public figures (and not-so-public figures writing anonymously on social media) continued to fight over the US transfer of executive governance, a representative of China's foreign ministry appraised the spectacle in its far-reaching, ricocheting implications. The United States, in recent years, Hua Chunying said, "has engaged in unilateralism, undermined multilateral cooperation, wantonly broken contracts (the country has so far withdrawn from more than ten international treaties and organizations), and posed the threat of sanctions."

Citing data collected in ten countries, Hua Chunying reported that some 50 percent of respondents (including among US allies) "think that the United States poses a major threat to their countries." The writer accurately concludes that US leaders seem to collect allies and enemies of convenience. Unfortunately, Americans "are standing on the wrong side of history." Their actions "run counter to friendship" between and among people of various countries—including among allies.

Among the United States' toxic diplomats is a Britain-born Washington insider and advisor to US partisans whose dabbling in US foreign affairs extends to the Yugoslavia years. Samantha Power has been credited with peddling "humanitarian interventionism" (breach of countries' sovereignty) to justify US violent aggression for economic gain and imperial domination. Power is a London, England, native and US Ivy League graduate who has been given thirty years to spread anachronistic (caveman) toxins. Her portfolio includes work with a transnational destabilizing NGO flying under the misnomer Carnegie Endowment for International *Peace* and the notorious *independent* US (spy) Agency for International Development (USAID).

The harm committed by clever Victoria(s) and Samantha(s) abroad (Nuland in Ukraine, Power in Yugoslavia) is the harm committed by the same shells and shell makers at home. Nongovernmental organizations and nonprofit profiteers notoriously commit multilayered (legalized) crimes of destabilizing countries and swindling governments and individuals at home and abroad. They create dependency and make people beg for their handouts. They avoid taxation that is shoved onto the shoulders of the masses. They plunder government treasuries, enriching and perpetuating themselves by means of extortionate government contracts.

Multicolored Killers at Home and Abroad

Regardless of the partisan angle or color coding of the person or persons heading the US government, the weakness of character (even cowardice) pervades all. US (debt) spending on weapons and troops, exceeding the next leading ten nations' spending in this area, neither strengthens the United States of America nor makes a leader or head of state strong.

US leaders' bullying, often accompanied by deadly aggression in missiles and deadly chemicals, stretching from Africa to Southern Asia (Pakistan to Sudan), manifests a character of moral weakness. US officials cling to a "superpower" status, or the appearance of superpower status, with brute force rather than the force of democratic ideals, the diplomacy of rational debate, discussion, and respectful give-and-take of conversation among equals. One author has observed that the "democratic ideals" of the United States have been thrown away, or consigned to the status of "life-support": imminent death.

The current crop of leaders and politicians aspiring to be US leaders may color-code themselves any way they choose. They may color code states of the United States as part of a pervasive gerrymandering scheme to obtain and remain in office. They are finaglers, tricksters lacking requisite merit, fitness, moral courage, and intellectual fortitude.

If a person cannot honestly earn, merit, or achieve a seat in public office on solid grounds—not merely on the basis of manufactured colors of geography or exaggerated colors of a race, creed, sex, gender, and various configurations and accidents of ancestry or orientation (none of which is relevant or indicative of individual accomplishment or creation, but may well invite distraction or malleability)—then that person does not deserve a chance to obtain or remain in public office.

Color them donkeys or elephants, the current crop of public officials in Washington and elsewhere and their revolving-door partners are *of a kind*, incestuously all the same. Failings in domestic and foreign affairs find root in the kleptocratic nature of US public officials. The weakness of a Biden or Trump, Reagan or Clinton, an Obama or Bush *is the weakening (chronic unpreparedness) of America.*

2

Part 2 Consequences

Unpreparedness, Loss of *Common Defense*
World, Domestic News Evidence of
Infantilism, Kleptocracy

A CONSEQUENCE OF UNITED States' spending more on its military than the combination of virtually all nations of the world and the concomitant neglect of the needs of the people of the United States is a terminally weakened America, an America in the throes of death.

Among *developed* countries (members of the Organization for Economic Cooperation and Development or OECD), the United States ranks *highest* in youth poverty, infant mortality, and incarceration. The United Nations High Commission for Refugees has found that conditions in Syrian refugee camps were better than those for the homeless in Los Angeles (now numbering nearly 60,000 in Los Angeles County). This is another layer of disgrace for America, where multibillionaires are lauded and further enriched by compromised officials; and thousands of Americans (including those who served in the same officials' manufactured theaters of war) are discarded to public streets and tunnels.

Chelala, César. "Quo Vadis, America? Enmeshing itself in unnecessary wars has weakened the United States considerably, both materially and in terms of international prestige." *The Globalist.* August 28, 2021 https://www.theglobalist.com/quo-vadis-america/

"Two decades on from9/11, the US has paid a heavy price for its War on Terror." RT news. September 11, 2021. https://www.rt.com/usa/534360-war-on-terror-cost-americans/

"Failure to Act" 2021Report: Economic Impacts of Status Quo Investment across Infrastructure Systems." American Society of Civil Engineers. https://infrastructurereportcard.org/the-impact/failure-to-act-report/

The Infrastructure Report Card "addresses the current infrastructure gaps between today's needs and investment and how they will affect the future productivity of industries, national competitiveness, and future costs to households." It updates the American Society of Civil Engineers Federal Transit Administration (ASCE FTA) economic series.[28]

"A Brief History of the Principle of National Banking in the United States." NIB Coalition. May 29, 2020. https://www.nibcoalition.com/a-brief-history-of-the-principle-of-national-banking-in-the-united-states

National Infrastructure Bank (NIB) Coalition says "The National Infrastructure Bank will create 25 million new jobs, pay Davis-Bacon[29] wages, and mandate 'Buy American' provisions."

Coalition for a National Infrastructure Bank. https://www.youtube.com/channel/UCAVaVupECCrwhXd1VY5Wn6Q

---

[28] "America's Infrastructure scores a C-," Report for America's Infrastructure 2021, American Society of Civil Engineers, ASCE Foundation, https://infrastructure reportcard.org/

[29] The Davis–Bacon Act of 1931 seems to concern itself with institutionalizing a more equal remuneration or application of "local prevailing wages" for people working on public works projects and people working on major structures, as federally funded contractors and subcontractors, in fields of construction, alteration, or repair (including painting and decorating). Wikipedia Foundation, updated June 21, 2022, https://en.wikipedia.org/wiki/Davis%E2%80%93Bacon_Act_of_1931

Common Defense, General Welfare
Breach of Promise

Priorities Chosen, Priorities Misplaced

Koshgarian. Lindsay. "The Pentagon Increase Is the Size of the Entire CDC Budget." National Priorities Project. May 14, 2021. https://www.nationalpriorities.org/blog/2021/05/14/pentagon-increase-size-entire-cdc-budget/

The author takes the view that the Biden administration budget is "stuck in an outdated version of what national security means." The Centers for Disease Control and Prevention "should be considered a vital part of (US) national security."

Friends Committee on National Legislation. "Pentagon Spending" August 26, 2020

https://www.fcnl.org/issues/us-wars-militarism/pentagon-spending
Congress and the Trump administration agreed to spend $746 billion on wars and the military for the fiscal year running through September 2020. That is nearly three-quarters of a trillion dollars; more than $2 billion every day; more than $1 million every minute. For every dollar US congresses and administrations budget for "preparing for and fighting wars," they "devote roughly 7 cents to diplomacy, peacebuilding, and development aid."

Mehta, Aaron and Joe Gould. "Biden requests $715B for Pentagon, hinting at administration's future priorities" Defense news. April 9, 2021. https://www.defensenews.com/breaking-news/2021/04/09/biden-requests-715b-for-pentagon-hinting-at-administrations-future-priorities/

US President Joe Biden's fiscal 2022 budget request asks for $753 billion in national security funding, an increase of 1.6 percent that includes $715 billion for the Defense Department.

Jagoda, Naomi. "IRS chief warns of unpaid taxes hitting $1 trillion." The Hill. April 13, 2021. https://thehill.com/policy/finance/548031-irs-chief-warns-of-unpaid-taxes-hitting-1-trillion

Siddique, Ashik. "COVID Shrank the Global Economy, but US Military Spending is Still More Than Next 11 Countries Combined." National Priorities. April 28, 2021. https://www.nationalpriorities. org/blog/2021/04/28/us-now-spends-more-military-next-11-countries-combined/

"Conflict, climate change, and COVID-19 drive extreme hunger" OXFAM. July 9, 2021. https://www.oxfamamerica.org/explore/stories/conflict-climate-change-and-covid-19-drive-extreme-hunger/

Reed, Kevin. "120 million people pushed to extreme poverty by COVID 19 pandemic." *World Socialist Web Site*, July 14, 2021. https://www.wsws.org/en/articles/2021/07/14/28e7-j14.html

Missing Essential Government Regulatory Operations
Failing Internal Structures

Green, Chris. "Massive chemical fire at Chemtool in Rockton could burn for days." *Rockford Register Star*. June 14, 2021 https://www.rrstar.com/story/news/2021/06/14/firefighters-battling-massive-industrial-blaze-rockton-illinois/7683567002/

"Huge blaze breaks out at Illinois chemical site after enormous explosion, locals evacuated." (VIDEO) RT news. June 14, 2021. https://www.rt.com/usa/526540-fire-chemical-plant-illinois-rockton/

Tickle, Jonny. "Russia had absolutely nothing to do with Colonial Pipeline cyberattack, despite Biden's claims to contrary, says Kremlin spokesman" RT reports. May 11, 2021. https://www.rt.com/russia/523485-colonial-pipeline-cyberattack-responsibility-denial-kremlin/

> One day after US President Joe Biden said that Russia has "some responsibility" for the (*also alleged*) ransomware attack that crippled America's Colonial Pipeline, the Kremlin has firmly denied Moscow had anything to do with the incident."

> Kremlin Representative Dmitry Peskov: "'Russia has nothing to do with this.'" Moreover, though "Moscow has been very willing to work with Washington in the area of cybercrime, "'the US has refused to cooperate in countering cybercrime.'" https://www.rt.com/russia/523485-colonial-pipeline-cyberattack-responsibility-denial-kremlin/

Rap Sheet
Background on Colonial Pipeline

- Twentieth-century infractions: Colonial pipeline charged with "gross negligence" and "violations of the Clean Water Act."
- Colonial Pipeline spills: "Seven in four years (three of which, 1996 to 1999, caused significant environmental damage to waterways in US Southeast.
- Twenty-first century: "Colonial had one of the largest gasoline spills, EVER, from a pipeline—at 1.2 million gallons, in a nature preserve in Huntersville, North Carolina." [30]

---

[30] "Colonial Pipeline," Wikipedia Foundation, (Last modified date March 13, 2022), https://en.wikipedia.org/wiki/Colonial_Pipeline

- Koch Industries PAC to federal candidates (2019–2020): $1,519,500
- Koch Industries (estimated) total lobbying expenditures (2020) $280,000
- Number 2 oil and gas recipient (2020) Joseph Robinette Biden Jr.: $1,638,621 [31]

Colonial Pipeline, headquartered in Alpharetta, Georgia, is owned by Koch Industries—Koch Industries Inc. revenue estimate for 2019: $115 billion—(a.k.a. Koch Capital Investments Company LLC, 28.09 percent stake ownership); South Korea's National Pension Service and Kohlberg Kravis Roberts (a.k.a. Keats Pipeline Investors LP, 23.44 percent stake ownership); Caisse de dépôt et placement du Québec (16.55 percent stake ownership via CDPQ Colonial Partners LP); Royal Dutch Shell (a.k.a. Shell Pipeline Company LP, 16.12 percent stake ownership); Industry Funds Management (a.k.a. IFM-US Colonial Pipeline 2 LLC, 15.80 percent stake ownership).[32], [33]

"Hazmat team responds to hydrochloric acid leak after 50-car train derails in Albert Lea, Minnesota." RT news. May 16, 2021" https://www.rt.com/usa/523947-minnesota-train-derail-acid-leak/

[31] "Koch Industries PAC Contributions to Federal Candidates," OpenSecrets (Federal Election Commission data released March 22, 2021, https://www.opensecrets.org/political-action-committees-pacs/C00236489/candidate-recipients/2020

[32] "Oil & Gas: Top Recipients," OpenSecrets, (Federal Election Commission data released May 23, 2022, donations during the 2021-2022 election cycle), https://www.opensecrets.org/industries./recips.php?ind=E01++

[33] "Client Profile: Colonial Pipeline," Calculations by OpenSecrets (most recent download April 22, 2022), Senate Office of Public Records data, https://www.opensecrets.org/federal-lobbying/clients/summary?cycle=2020&id=D000064648

Rap Sheet
Background: Union Pacific

- 2004 (June 28, San Antonio): Train crashed into idle BNSF train in a San Antonio suburb, a derailment causing the puncturing of a 90-ton tank car carrying liquefied chlorine, a toxic "yellow cloud" forming that killed three people, caused 43 hospitalizations, and cleanup and property damage costs exceeding $7 million.
- 2007 (September 4, Sergeant Bluff, Iowa): 16-car (est.) derailment, most carrying salt that spilled into snow-like piles.
- 2008 (Eugene, Oregon, study finding): Century-old railroad yard seeps "mostly petroleum hydrocarbons, industrial solvents, and metals into groundwater."
- 2012 (June 24, near Goodwell (Texas County), Oklahoma): Trains collided head-on, leaving three crew members dead and property damage estimated at $15 million.
- 2012 (November 15): Train struck a parade float in Midland, Texas, killing four, injuring sixteen people on the float.
- 2013 (May 25, Chaffee, Missouri): Train collided with a BNSF train, leaving seven people injured, causing a fire and damages exceeding $10 million, and partially collapsing Missouri Route M overpass.
- 2016 (June 3, Columbia River Gorge near Mosier, Oregon): 96-car oil train derailment; 11 derailing causing fire to train; and Bakken crude oil spill of 42,000 US gal (160 m3), some into the Columbia River.
- 2018 (January, Portland, Oregon): Former waste water operator at Union Pacific Albina Yard employed by the railroad's contractor, Mott MacDonald, negligently released thousands of gallons of oil into the environment.
- 2019 (September 7, Portland, Oregon): Remotely operated derailment and crash traversing broken rails: two locomotives and three tank cars carrying liquefied petroleum gas derailed

crashing into an overpass support column at the Albina Yard, leaving four lanes unsafe, others in permanent disrepair.

- 2020 (May, North Portland, Oregon): Derailment damages a different overpass, safety concerns persisted.
- 2021(May 15, Albert Lea, Minnesota, near Goose Lake): Derailment of around twenty-eight cars "carrying mixed commodities …, leaving dozens of cars piled up on top of one another—some leaking hydrochloric acid."

The Union Pacific Railroad (legally Union Pacific Railroad Company and Union Pacific, Parent company Union Pacific Corporation, headquartered in Omaha, Nebraska) is the second largest railroad in the United States after BNSF. It is a freight-hauling railroad operating routes in 23 US states west of Chicago and New Orleans. Union Pacific and BNSF Railway (Burlington Northern and Santa Fe Railway, parent company Berkshire Hathaway) have a duopoly on transcontinental freight rail lines in the western United States. Union Pacific was founded in 1862 as Union Pacific Rail Road, part of the First Transcontinental Railroad project later known as the Overland Route. [34], [35], [36]

Hydrochloric acid is an important laboratory reagent and industrial chemical classified as a strong acid. It is a colorless solution used in many industrial processes such as refining metal. Major Hydrochloric acid worldwide producers (headquartered in the United States) are Dow Chemical (headquartered in Midland, Michigan) and Georgia Gulf Corporation (Axiall Corporation, headquartered in Atlanta, Georgia).[37]

---

[34] "Union Pacific Corporation," Wikipedia Foundation (Last modified May 14, 2022), https://en.wikipedia.org/wiki/Union_Pacific_Corporation

[35] "Union Pacific Railroad," Wikipedia Foundation (Last modified June 5, 2022), https://en.wikipedia.org/wiki/Union_Pacific_Railroad#Notable_accidents

[36] "BNSF Railway," (Wikipedia Foundation (Last modified June 17, 2022), https://en.wikipedia.org/wiki/BNSF_Railway

[37] "Hydrochloric acid," Wikipedia Foundation (Last modified June 14, 2022), https://en.wikipedia.org/wiki/Hydrochloric_acid

Galvan, Alfonzo and Philip Joens, Robin Opsahl, and the Associated Press. "No time 'to take anything': Evacuation order still in place for many in Sibley [Iowa] after train derails, smoke billows into sky." Des Moines Register. May 17, 2021. https://www.desmoinesregister.com/story/news/2021/05/17/iowa-train-derailment-sibley-evacuation-order-remains-explosion-threat-nullified/5125238001/

Kordenbrock, Mike "Multiple people injured in Hi-Line train derailment remained hospitalized Sunday." Billings Gazette. September 26, 2021. https://billingsgazette.com/news/local/multiple-people-injured-in-hi-line-train-derailment-remained-hospitalized-Sunday/article_f3af200e-21a3-500f-94dc-db1a0241f94c.html#tracking-source=home-top-story

Niemuth, Niles. "Deadly train derailment in Montana exposes decrepit state of US infrastructure." World Socialist Web Site. September 29, 2021. https://www.wsws.org/en/articles/2021/09/29/pers-s29.html

Franklin, Jonathan and JC Whittington, Matthew Torres, Tom Dempsey, Nick Boykin (WUSA9). "Collapsed pedestrian bridge given 'poor condition' rating at most recent inspection, officials say. Mayor Muriel Bowser said the bridge was structurally sound early on Wednesday after the incident, a misstatement that now has been admitted by her office." WUSA9. June 23, 2021. https://www.wusa9.com/article/news/local/dc/pedestrian-bridge-collapse-dc-fire-northeast-dc-minor-injuries/65-ef75a077-030a-4bae-879d-010559eb2e27

Bradbury, Shelly. "Trial starts for I-70 truck driver who caused deadly 28-vehicle crash in Lakewood: Rogel Lazaro Aguilera-Mederos faces 41 charges in 2019 crash that killed 4, injured 6." Denver Post. September 23, 2021. https://www.denverpost.com/2021/09/23/truck-driver-trial-fatal-crash-i-70/

Blaskey, Sarah and Aaron Leibowitz. "'Major error' was flagged in 2018 inspection report of collapsed building [Champlain Towers South Condo in Surfside] near Miami Beach." Miami Herald. June 26, 2021 https://www.miamiherald.com/news/local/community/miami-dade/miami-beach/article252385083.html

> Thursday June 24, 2021 Surfside (near Miami), Florida—an occupied 12-story condominium tower in disrepair falls down. By Saturday several people were confirmed dead, more than a hundred were missing, and fire and smoke were preventing rescue efforts.

Bynum, Russ and Freida Frisaro "'Deep fire' slowing rescue effort at collapsed Florida condo." Associated Press June 26, 2021. https://apnews.com/article/miami-building-collapses-4e872d03fc3210b49c60e6a275f2e860

"Death toll in Miami building collapse rises to 9 as rescue teams keep working 'non-stop.'" RT news June 27, 2021. https://www.rt.com/usa/527731-death-toll-miami-collapse-rises/

"Engineer warned of 'major structural damage' years before Florida condo complex collapsed—media." RT news June 26, 2021. https://www.rt.com/usa/527670-florida-condo-collapse-engineer-structural-damage/

"'Things are going to get more difficult': Death toll in Miami building collapse rises to 4 as officials report 159 missing." RT newsJune 25, 2021. https://www.rt.com/usa/527578-florida-surfside-collapse-deaths-missing/

Robertson, Linda and Douglas Hanks, Samantha J. Gross, and Martin Vassolo. "Surfside collapse sparks discussion about inspection reforms: After Surfside collapse, Miami-Dade governments check on older buildings, discuss reform." *Miami Herald*. June 28, 2021. https://www.miamiherald.com/news/local/community/miami-dade/miami-beach/article252425378.html

"Five sailors died when a helicopter crashed in the Pacific Ocean off of Southern California." Military Network (Associated Press). September

5, 2021 https://www.military.com/daily-news/2021/09/05/us-navy-ids-5-killed-helicopter-crash-off-california.html

Pattern:

- 2019: five severe incidents
- 2020: nine severe incidents
- 2021: eleven severe incidents

  Eleven navy-manned aircraft crashed in 2021; "number of incidents per 100,000 flight hours has been steadily climbing over the past three years." (Naval Safety Center statistics) Military dot com https://www.military.com/daily-news/2021/09/07/navy-helicopter-rotor-struck-carrier-deck-causing-crash-killed-five.html https://www.military.com/topics/aviation-accidents

Toropin, Konstantin. "Safety Report Urges Aviators to Show 'Moral Courage' and Recognize Shortcomings." Military Network. August 6, 2021. https://www.military.com/daily-news/2021/08/06/safety-report-urges-aviators-show-moral-courage-and-recognize-shortcomings.html

Erblat, Austen "Small plane crashes near Publix, killing pilot in training." South Florida Sun Sentinel. May 12, 2020. https://www.sun-sentinel.com/local/broward/miramar/fl-ne-miramar-plane-crash-20200512-6v54bjgez5cvrc7sv7paub7uim-story.html

Erblat, Austen. "Small plane crashes on landing in Fort Lauderdale." South Florida Sun Sentinel. September 26, 2021. https://www.sun-sentinel.com/local/broward/fort-lauderdale/fl-ne-plane-crash-bahamas-20210926-2sezgzcd5zbvbcuej4424i75v4-story.html

"Senate releases damning report on Capitol riot: Intel ignored, officers undertrained & underequipped, leaders & backup missing." RT news. May 8, 2021. https://www.rt.com/usa/526012-senate-report-capitol-riot/

"'Over 1,000 businesses' potentially affected by US cyberattack. Press TV news. July 3, 2021 https://www.presstv.ir/Detail/2021/07/03/661454/-Over-1,000-businesses--potentially-affected-by-US-cyberattack

Losses: Air, Land, Water

"US Navy's explosive test off Florida coast triggers 3.9-magnitude 'quake' as world's most expensive warship undergoes shock trial." RT news. July 17, 2021 https://www.rt.com/usa/529460-navy-carrier-explosion-test/ de Vries, Daniel. "New York's Ida [Hurricane] disaster: A social crime in the center of world capitalism." September 4, 2021 *World Socialist Web Site* opinion. https://www.wsws.org/en/articles/2021/09/04/pers-s04.html

> The record rainfall that overwhelmed much of the Northeastern United States … left at least 48 dead and millions more grappling with the fallout from the historic flooding.
>
> The remnants of Hurricane Ida dropped more than 2 inches (5 cm) of rain on 60 million people throughout the region, with densely populated portions of New York and New Jersey recording up to 9 inches (23 cm) overnight. In New York City's Central Park, the storm gushed 3.15 inches (8 cm) of water in just one hour, blowing away the previous record set just 11 days earlier.

Boyd-Barrett, Claudia. "Some rural California communities have waited nearly a decade for state regulators to repair their tainted drinking-water systems." *High Country News*. May 5, 2021 https://www.hcn.org/articles/south-water-im-scared-of-getting-sick-from-the-water

Some rural California communities have waited nearly a decade for state regulators to repair their tainted drinking-water systems.

Berlin, Carly. "The multibillion dollar question: What will it take to fix the South's broken water systems?" *Southerly Magazine.* April 15, 2021. https://southerlymag.org/2021/04/15/the-multibillion-dollar-question-what-will-it-take-for-the-south-to-get-clean-water/

"How long has that water already been in the system? Water stays in the pipes longer in shrinking cities – a challenge for public health"[38] *The Conversation.* May 24, 2019. Martin La Monica, Deputy Editor for science coverage. https://theconversation.com/water-stays-in-the-pipes-longer-in-shrinking-cities-a-challenge-for-public-health-116119

Losses: Health, Medical, Trust

"Record in Overdose." We the People Press TV July 28, 2021. https://www.presstv.ir/Detail/2021/07/28/663232/Record-in-Overdose

The US has seen a sharp spike in the number of overdose deaths across the country since the coronavirus pandemic began.

According to official estimates, deaths caused by drug overdose hit a record 93 thousand people last year.

The official figure translates to nearly 255 deaths every single day caused by drug abuse. This "We the People" episode examines repercussions and societal

---

[38] Authors Nancy Love, University of Michigan professor of civil and environmental engineering; Richard Jackson, University of California–Los Angeles professor emeritus of environmental health sciences; Shawn P. McElmurry, Wayne State University associate professor of civil and environmental engineering; Editor Beth Daley

consequences of addiction. "Has government done enough to address the issue?"

Kutz, Jessica. "Foreign-born doctors fill physician shortages in the West; Some find a permanent home; others languish in a visa holding pattern." *High Country News*. February 25, 2021. https://www.hcn.org/issues/53.3/south-public-health-foreign-born-doctors-fill-physician-shortages-in-the-west

"Malfunction at the podium? Psaki announces vaccines 'can still kill you' in eyebrow-raising slip-up." July 15, 2021. https://www.rt.com/usa/529303-psaki-vaccines-kill-gaffe/

Morrison, Sara. "Millions of people got Covid-19 tests through Walgreens. Their information wasn't adequately protected: How Walgreens' sloppy Covid-19 test registration system exposed patient data." Vox news. September 13, 2021. https://www.vox.com/recode/22623871/walgreens-covid-test-site-data-vulnerability

"NY governor to monitor whether to bring in National Guard medics to replace fired unvaccinated doctors as mandate deadline expires." RT news. September 28, 2021. https://www.rt.com/usa/536044-ny-emergency-vaccine-mandate/

"The Deadly Shortage of Healthcare Workers Has One Main Cause ... and it's not COVID." Brown and Barron LLC. February 3, 2022. https://www.brownbarron.com/blog/2022/february/the-deadly-shortage-of-healthcare-workers-has-on/

Under the United States' corporate for-profit healthcare system, the drive for higher and higher profits demands reduction of medical personnel. Thus, America's hospitals and nursing homes were undergoing "a deadly staffing crisis" long before the pandemic; and in the midst of the crisis, the pandemic is "not solely to blame." In nursing homes lacking essential staffing, patient deaths that would have been *avoidable* are *unavoidable*. The nursing shortage "is a self-inflicted" wound (emphasis added).

"Major Shortages of Healthcare Workers Nationwide Projected by 2026." Healthcare Staffing Report Staffing Industry Analysts. October 14, 2021. https://www2.staffingindustry.com/Editorial/Healthcare-Staffing-Report/Oct.-14-2021/Major-shortages-of-healthcare-workers-nationwide-projected-by-2026

- Half of the states of the United States will sustain significant shortages in nursing staffs by 2026.
- Primary care will be increasingly provided by people who are not physicians.
- The need for mental health professionals will increase by 10 percent.

San Felice, Selene. "Biden and DeSantis [Florida Governor Ronald Dion DeSantis] snipe over Florida's COVID response." *Axios*. August 5, 2021. https://www.axios.com/local/tampa-bay/2021/08/05/joe-biden-ron-desantis-florida-covid

Gonzalez, Oriana. "Biden admin threatens [Arizona Governor Douglas Anthony Ducey Jr] to take back Arizona's COVID aid over anti-mask rules." *Axios*. January 14, 2022. https://www.axios.com/biden-treasury-arizona-federal-covid-aid-masks-72001cd2-d771-4fbe-bab1-dbadb011d8b4.html

Frazier, Kierra. "Students across US walkout of classes to demand safer COVID protocols." *Axios*. January 15, 2022. https://www.axios.com/students-walkout-classes-covid-protocols-a3b7c026-d598-4555-9452-0d86c212cf44.html

Losses: Education, Schooling

Smith, Morgan. "In Texas, Efforts to Raise Teacher Certification Standards Falter: For-profit teacher certification companies are flourishing in Texas. But as the industry grows, so do questions about the state's ability to control the quality of training the programs provide." *Texas Tribune*. August 22, 2014. https://www.texastribune.org/2014/08/22/raising-teacher-certification-standards-obstacles/

Van Overschelde, James P. "Eliminating roadblocks to improving educator preparation in Texas." *Texas Tribune* TribTalk. October 26, 2015. https://www.tribtalk.org/2015/10/26/eliminating-roadblocks-to-improving-educator-preparation-in-texas/

Johnson, Alex. "Fifteen educators and staff from Florida's Miami-Dade School district die within ten days as COVID-19 deaths skyrocket across state." *World Socialist Web Site*. September 7, 2019 https://www.wsws.org/en/articles/2021/09/08/miam-s08.html

Lopez, Brian. "Coronavirus in Texas: The pandemic's toll on educators has made Texas' teacher shortage worse: Teachers report being spread thin by the demands of remote learning and exhausted by the constant health concerns." *Texas Tribune*. September 9, 2021. https://www.texastribune.org/2021/09/09/texas-teachers-shortage-covid-19/

Lieberman, Mark. "How Staff Shortages Are Crushing Schools." Education Week. October 15, 2021 https://www.edweek.org/leadership/how-staff-shortages-are-crushing-schools/2021/10
An Education Week survey of teacher staffing shortages (reported by responding school district leaders and principals) showed

- 37 percent "moderate" staffing shortages
- 25 percent "severe" shortages
- 15 percent "very severe" shortages
- 5 percent no staffing issues

Pandey, Erica. "America's teacher shortage will outlast the pandemic." *Axios.* November 15, 2021. https://www.axios.com/teacher-labor-shortage-outlast-pandemic-d0953fec-115a-4d19-82a9-6fed552f29f9.html

Donaldson, Emily and Talia Richman. "In this Texas district, the superintendent subs and a teacher drives the bus to keep kids in school: Terrell staff members pull double duty to confront 'Swiss cheese schooling' as the pandemic lingers." *Dallas Morning News.* February 4, 2022.

https://www.dallasnews.com/news/education/2022/02/04/in-this-texas-district-the-superintendent-subs-a-teacher-drives-the-bus-to-keep-kids-in-school/

Losses: Nourishment, Shelter

Stebbins, Samuel. "Poverty level: These are the cities in each state hit the hardest by extreme poverty 24/7: 43.5 million Americans living in poverty." *USA Today.* December 2, 2020
https://www.usatoday.com/story/money/2020/12/02/cities-hit-hardest-by-extreme-poverty-in-every-state/115073018/

"Report found that 580,466 people experienced homelessness in the United States on a single night in 2020, an increase of 12,751 people, or 2.2 percent, from 2019." Homelessness in America. March 18, 2021. https://endhomelessness.org/homelessness-in-america/homelessness-statistics/state-of-homelessness-2020/

> Seventeen out of every 10,000 people in the United States were experiencing homelessness on a single night in January 2019 during HUD's Annual Point-in-Time Count. These 567,715 people represent a cross-section of America. They are associated with every region of

the country, family status, gender category, and racial/ethnic group.

"State of Homelessness in 2021: Statistics, Analysis, & Trends Federal Data Shows Steady Pre-COVID-19 Increase in Homelessness." Security dot org, April 12, 2021. https://www.security.org/resources/homeless-statistics

Kilduff, Lillian and Beth Jarosz. "How Many People in the United States Are Experiencing Homelessness?" Population Reference Bureau (PRB), September 22, 2020. https://www.prb.org/resources/how-many-people-in-the-united-states-are-experiencing-homelessness/

In most cities of the United States, homeless populations have increased. Some cities have experienced "double-digit increases in just a couple of years." Thirty-six of America's cities' homelessness exceeded the average 10 percent.

Goncalves, Delia. "'She wasn't just the lady under the bridge': DC woman loses life during Wednesday's winter storm." WUSA9. February 19, 2021. https://www.wusa9.com/article/news/local/dc-homeless-woman-loses-life-during-winter-storm/65-dfe148da-39ba-4e11-b687-5c471f3e4b4b

Fifty-eight-year-old Angela Hill had lived under the I-295 overpass in Southeast Washington DC, for nearly ten years. Something went wrong.

Thompson, Jonathan. "Solving the West's housing crisis: We need to care for the priced-out average worker or something is bound to break." *High Country News* Opinion. May 11, 2021. https://www.hcn.org/articles/opinion-economy-solving-the-wests-housing-crisis

Losses: Work, Workers

Savage, Erin. "Collapse of the coal industry: Problems and recommendations." *The Appalachian Voice*, June 8, 2021. https://appvoices.org/2021/06/08/collapse-coal/.

Utilities are diversifying away from coal. Mining companies that have long made their only profit on this single commodity are collapsing into bankruptcy. Some company owners are "just walking away from mine sites …, leaving workers, communities, and regulators to pick up the pieces."

Regulators have failed to keep up with the collapse because they have been denied the necessary government funding and legal tools "to address growing problems of scarred landscapes and polluted waters." There is "an urgent need for regulatory action to restore lands and waters." Immediate action by the "Office of Surface Mining Reclamation & Enforcement" (OSMRE) is imperative.

Horseherder, Nicole. "A just and equitable transition is needed to honor the sacrifices made by Navajo and Hopi." *Arizona Mirror*. June 14, 2021. https://www.azmirror.com/2021/06/14/a-just-and-equitable-transition-is-needed-to-honor-the-sacrifices-made-by-navajo-and-hopi/

Thompson, Jonathan. "Put unemployed miners and drillers back to work in restoration: There's economic development in reclaiming coal mines and plugging idled wells." *High Country News*, Opinion, February 23, 2021. https://www.hcn.org/articles/writers-on-the-range-economy-put-unemployed-miners-and-drillers-back-to-work-in-restoration

Extremism: Anarchism
A Strange Relationship
with Language

A MONG AMERICANS, THERE is a strange relationship with language *and therefore with culture or cultures*. There is a concerted contemptuousness, a boastful ignorance and narrow-mindedness, a deliberate abusiveness in Americans' approach to the dominant language of the United States and to languages of other countries. I am labeling this attitude *infantilism*. It is a dangerous childishness that weakens the United States and its citizens and has deleterious effects on relations between the United States and other countries.

Arrogant Resistance to Language Proficiency
National and International

English is the "official language" of some fifty-nine sovereign states and twenty-seven non-sovereign entities throughout the world.

In the United States, English is the *de facto* (commonly spoken) language, but it is not the country's official *nationwide* language under law. In several of the states, English has been codified as the official language, but the law does not carry throughout the nation. As of 2019, thirty-one of the fifty states had decreed English as the state's official language under law:

1. Alabama	2. Alaska	3. Arizona

4. Arkansas	14. Kansas	24. Oklahoma
5. California	15. Kentucky	25. South Carolina
6. Colorado	16. Massachusetts	26. South Dakota
7. Florida	17. Mississippi	27. Tennessee
8. Georgia	18. Missouri	28. Utah
9. Hawaii	19. Montana	29. Virginia
10. Idaho	20. Nebraska	30. West Virginia
11. Illinois	21. New Hampshire	31. Wyoming
12. Indiana	22. North Carolina	
13. Iowa	23. North Dakota	

In the 116th Congress and many preceding Congresses, a member of the House and the Senate has pushed for and failed to succeed in passing legislation making the United States' dominant language (English) its official nationwide language under law. Congressman Steven Arnold King of Iowa on February 6, 2019, introduced the English Language Unity Act of 2019 (H.R.997) that garnered twenty-seven cosponsors before being buried in the "Subcommittee on Immigration and Citizenship." If the bill had passed, it would have established "English as the official language of the United States," together with rules for implementing and enforcing the law.[39] On March 6, 2019, Senator James Mountain Inhofe of Oklahoma introduced "S.678," the companion English Language Unity Act of 2019. This bill garnered only three cosponsors before dying in the Committee on Homeland Security and Governmental Affairs.[40]

Why do pre- and post-secondary institutions not teach, correct English language usage, and insist on students and teachers' speaking the English language (standard, grammatically correct English) correctly? Why are speakers of incorrect English hired or given contract positions in broadcasting or in other on-air media venues?

---

[39] "English Language Unity Act of 2019," 116th Congress (2019-2020), All Information (Except Text) for H.R.997, Library of Congress, https://www.congress.gov/bill/116th-congress/house-bill/997/all-info

[40] "English Language Unity Act of 2019," 116th Congress (2019-2020), All Information (Except Text) for S.678, Library of Congress, https://www.congress.gov/bill/116th-congress/senate-bill/678/all-info

DR. CAROLYN LADELLE BENNETT

Language (*one language*) is essential to *oneness*. Those who stand firm in their language and allegiance to country have no fear of others and other languages. To love and take pride in one's language and culture is not to disdain other languages and cultures; nor is it to discount the lasting imprint of British imperialism. Countries that seem to have a clear sense of self and pride in their culture have inscribed in law official languages. Among these countries are: the Republic of Ireland (Irish), Ethiopia (Amharic), Iran (Persian, or Farsi) Philippines (Filipino), Russia (Russian), Ukraine (Ukrainian with Russian widely spoken), France (French), Spain (Spanish), the Czech Republic (Czech), Pakistan (Urdu), Haiti (Haitian Creole and French).

Instead of embracing language as a unifier of nation and people, many leading American politicians, public figures, and users of various forms of media seem to prefer the use of language as a hammer and divider of the nation and its people, as well as a weapon against other nations and leaders. There is a kind of anarchy (and infantilism) in the American approach that, as one historian has observed, ensures constant animosity and thus prevents the accomplishment of essential work, essential progress at home and abroad.

Language Abuse, Misuse, Vulgarization, Weaponization

People employed by the US government, even those representing the US abroad are the most arrogant and worst modelers of written and spoken language—and communication more generally. Too often, and surprisingly, public officials engage in coarse speech. Offensiveness (mudslinging, insult, trash-talking) is often heard from members of the US Congress: among fellow members, and between members of the legislature and officials in other branches of government. It is heard in interactions between top officials in Washington and top officials in individual US states. It is heard in US officials' language when in discussions with or in reference to officials of other countries. People in broadcast and print media on and offline copy the pattern. The effect is astounding, off-putting, and utterly undignified in its *childishness*. How are the young to learn the right way when the old and higher-ups display the wrong way?

Entering the first spring of the new White House, the spokeswoman Jen Psaki boasted that the relatively new US president had "no regrets" about calling Russian Federation president Vladimir Putin "a killer." The utterances were improper on so many levels: the press's framing of the question, the president's response to the question, the White House representative's further comment, and the later commentary by the US president. The press planted the toxin by posing an unproven fact and then suggesting a conclusion from the unproven fact and asking the US president to agree with the conclusion they had drawn from their manufactured premise. Round and round they go. Repeating and echoing toxins, deepening animosities.

Deutsche Welle news reported: "When asked (by ABC news) if he thinks Putin, who has been accused of poisoning political opponents, is a 'killer,' Biden replied, 'I do.'"

Global News and other sources then published headlines attributing to the Russian leader the words, "'He who said it, did it.'" (Andrew Osborn and Tom Balmforth, Reuters, March 18, 2021 updated March 19, 2021).

At later press conference in Geneva, Switzerland, in June of 2021, as the world faced unchecked animosity between major nuclear powers, the press continued to push its toxic back-and-forth "killer" points, this time eliciting "laughter" from the US president (as insane as Obama's secretary of state Hillary Clinton's laughter following the assassination of Libyan president Muammar al-Qaddafi). "Why would I bring it up again?" the US president is reported saying.

How does this press-presidential pageantry advance world progress, improve relations among nations, or prevent a nuclear winter? It doesn't.

It accomplishes quite the opposite. The infantile regress-causing battle between US leaders and foreign leaders is the same pattern that is on display among Washington inmates. "If you see anybody from that Cabinet in a restaurant, in a department store, at a gasoline station, you get out and you create a crowd and you push back on them and you tell them they're not welcome anymore, anywhere." This was the fighting language of one of America's entrenched members of the US Congress during the second year of former US president Donald Trump's tenure.

The speaker was US representative Maxine Waters. She was later rebuked by at least one of her congressional colleagues who cautioned of dangers of "resorting to violence, harassment and intimidation." Then-Speaker of the House Paul Ryan said (*correctly*) that the congresswoman's words were out of place and that she should apologize.

President Trump matched Waters' dishonorable utterances by describing her as "an extraordinarily low-IQ person" who had "called for harm to supporters." In his made-for-cheap- television style, the president flung a cliché: "Be careful what you wish for."

Waters attempted to slither out of her dishonorable performance by redefining terms (in the Washington mode of *humanitarian* killers). "We have to tell people the difference between violence and incivility and protesting," Waters was quoted saying. Not stopping there, she issued a denial: "I did not threaten [Trump] constituents and supporters," then mangled her denial: "*I do that all the time*, but I didn't do that that time." She seemed to have been playing to her Los Angeles audience, who were heard laughing mindlessly at her performance.[41]

In the final days of the Trump presidency, aggression came to Capitol Hill. The day after the infamous January 6, 2021, event, then-White House press secretary Kayleigh McEnany led a press conference,

---

[41] Megan Keller, "Maxine Waters mocks: I threaten Trump supporters 'all the time,'" September 10, 2018, The Hill, https://thehill.com/homenews/house/405877-maxine-waters-i-threaten-trump-supporters-all-the-time/

beginning with the meaningless opening often used by the Washington entrenched, "Let me be clear." McEnany went on to assure his audience that "The violence we saw ... at our nation's Capitol was appalling, reprehensible, and antithetical to the *American* way (and) We condemn it—the President and this administration—in the strongest possible terms." As with Waters, McEnany attempted to duck and deny responsibility for violence or for inciting violence. He said the incident involved "a group of violent rioters undermining the legitimate First Amendment rights of the many thousands who came to peacefully have their voices heard in our nation's capital." McEnany seemed to dismiss all those deaths in Western Asia on orders, policy and legislation of US administrations and congresses when he declared: "the core value of our administration...is the idea that all citizens have the right to live in safety, peace, and freedom." The hills are alive, and the forest echoes *Kumbayah*?

Violence invites violence. Language of aggression invites violence at home or abroad, in domestic or international affairs, making unity and working relations impossible. To suggest otherwise is just baby talk— an adult's refusal to take responsibility for personal and professional behavior, the failure to uphold the dignity and due diligence required by the office or position.

John Jay, in the founding era, spoke of the wisdom and goodness of those who served in government, in the congresses. One cannot make this statement today. "Incivility and dysfunction in Congress is a national crisis," wrote former historian of the US House of Representatives, Ray Smock. In past generations, members of Congress "had respect for Congress as a constitutional institution; they respected its traditions, mores, and rules." But today's "polarized, highly-partisan members of Congress are less interested in learning the rules and traditions." They often see these "as impediments rather than as tools for governing."

Members can be not only "uncivil to one another." But even worse, they can be "uncivil to the very institution of Congress." What Smock

DR. CAROLYN LADELLE BENNETT

observes in today's government—in the conditions, work ethic, relations between and among officials—"is akin to anarchy." *Anything goes*. It is, he says, "the ultimate expression of incivility."[42]

In the Executive Branch of the US government, one woman has excelled in brazen impropriety and yet has been allowed to hold almost continuous positions in the area of US international affairs. She is a card-carrying member of the Washington entrenched corps of revolving-door inmates. While in the Obama state department (before moving on to the Biden state department), she was prone to unspeakable vulgarity in language and onsite provocation of violence related to other countries and leaders. Victoria Jane Nuland's vulgarism and destructiveness have gone unchecked by Washington's more senior officials. In a 2014 telephone conversation, Nuland and US ambassador to Ukraine Geoffrey Pyatt reportedly discussed their active interference in Ukraine's electoral affairs. When the discussion turned to the European Union's objection to playing their game of meddling in Ukraine's sovereign affairs, Nuland notoriously commented using a gross profanity against the European Union (four-lettered … the EU); and her colleague, Mr. Pyatt, seemed to share her vulgarism with his response. "Oh, exactly …"

Whatever the political party label, whatever the ideological bent or pretense, the language of US foreign policy and dealings with other countries is the language of belligerence and insult, as illustrated in Nuland's insult. She effectively committed an offense against twenty-seven European Union member states (population 445,834,883), stretching more than 1,544,408.634 square miles (or 4 million km²).

Who cares? On February 13, 2021, the Biden government officially invited Victoria Nuland to serve in his government—a person who had openly and repeatedly disgraced both the official position and US public office and further decreased the standing of the United States

[42] Ray Smock is director of the Robert C. Byrd Center for Legislative Studies at Shepherd University, Shepherdstown, West Virginia. He was historian of the US House of Representatives from 1983 to 1995.

in world affairs and, of course, made it impossible to carry on honest, trustworthy, and effective (i.e., good) relations with other nations and peoples. The US Senate acquiesced to Biden's decision and approved the nomination of a manifestly inappropriate individual to assume the position of undersecretary of state.

Reflecting on the 2021 transfer of government in the United States and the insults being hurled against the leadership of the Russian Federation, Brian Cloughley wrote that hopes had been dashed of anyone who expected the tone of US foreign policy to change. "Insulting Russia's leader, telling the Germans how to run their economy, and refusing a reasonable British extradition request (tormenting Julian Assange and demanding his extradition from England to the United States while refusing to extradite to England an American, Anne Sacoolas, who fled England after her dangerous driving killed teenager Harry Dunn) are all in a day's work for the White House, which appears to be oblivious to the damage that is being done to broad US interests."[43]

Reflecting also on the Biden debut, which wasn't really his government debut, and Biden's slanderous words, a Strategic Culture Foundation editorial concluded that, as "piles of dead bodies (lay) … mountainous… under the feet of American politicians," the Biden performance early in his presidency betrays a monstrously cavalier "arrogance and ignorance of an American political class who, on the one hand make … accusations against President Putin based on flimsy rumors, such as the alleged poisoning of conman Alexei Navalny and, at the same time, show a lack of decency or decorum by bandying about vulgar labels …"

Foul Language, Fighting Words, Deliberate Ignorance

Language is a discipline like any area of study. Not unlike science or mathematics, language also teaches discipline as a way of being. In its

---

[43] Writer Brian Cloughley was a deputy head of the UN military mission in Kashmir and Australian defense attaché in Pakistan.

limitless varieties and nuances, language opens the mind to innumerous discriminating choices of tone and term. Language disciplines and liberates. Any individual in any context has a wide variety of choices and opportunities not to insult or attack. Nevertheless, many individuals with microphones and university platforms in America choose to insult and attack. There was a time when the innate qualities of language were appreciated and institutions of higher learning and organizations carrying news and information to general audiences demanded and strictly enforced proper standards of voice, text, and images. In today's anarchic, nihilistic mentality, raunchy is "righteous," and anything goes.

Many people found it easy to apply *narcissism* to Donald Trump, not only because he trumpeted himself but because his name was plastered on huge structures all over the world, including in the United States. However, the term applies equally to public figures and politicians offstage and onstage (on camera or on social media platforms, in scripted public hearings or pressers, or, more insidiously, behind the scenes of media and government). Rule makers wrapped in a tattered flag of twisted *rights* flaunt rule breaking. Often under a god of their making—*anything goes*. Anarchism meets narcissism in an arrested stage of development.

American university faculties endorse the language of reductionist, rude rappers (hip-hoppers) and profanity-spewing professors. A Rutgers University tenured professor is heard saying and is later quoted by press organizations throughout the world: "We got to take white people out." The Daily Mail (UK) report of the woman's language laced with broken English and vulgarisms revealed a face of violent obsession and fanaticism:

> "Their ('white' people's) projects are not so sophisticated"
> …; "'we' (unknown we) could help to figure out an end
> and a way to the other side of this gargantuan historical
> tragedy that is 'white supremacy'… Despite what white

people think of themselves, they do not define the laws of eternity."

The madness continued. "The thing I want to say to you is, 'We got to take these (really bad plural word I'll not print) out' but like we can't say that," she said. Then, contradicting herself, having committed an act of violence in her language, she is quoted saying that "... she 'doesn't believe in a project of violence.'" The Brittney Cooper case is another manifestation of the substandard state of US institutions of *higher* learning, officials' careless approval, even celebration, of ignorance and vulgarity among their faculties setting the example for the young. This self-styled "victim" spewing profanity, and profiteering on blaming others for perceived or manufactured injury or injustices has been given voice in the pages of America's major print and broadcast media such as the *New York Times* and National Public Radio.

It is of interest that the same category of "white" men Cooper insults and blames for her problems (or psychosis) are men who conceived land grant universities and federally chartered universities from which she took academic degrees. Over two centuries, Howard University has received appropriations in the federal budget. Emory University, founded by "white" people (1836), bears the name of Methodist Episcopal Church bishop John Emory. The Morrill Act was passed in the Thirty-seventh Congress and signed into law by the 16th US President, Abraham Lincoln in 1862. The act gave every US state and territory 30,000 acres per member of Congress to be used to establish land grant universities. Congressman Justin Smith Morrill of Vermont had introduced the original bill. The idea of US Federally Chartered Universities originated during the administration of the 4th US President, James Madison.

The profiteering "righteous" "oppressed" "victims" might consider owning up to the full account of their ancestral imprint. American researchers such as Henry Louis Gates and others have studied the "colors" of slaveholders and found free "black" people in America participated in the buying and selling of "other 'black' people." This practice of buying and selling began around 1654 and reportedly continued through the American Civil War. Moreover, according to Gates, there was further evidence that slave owning lent standing. Negro slave owners, at least some of them, believed that copying the slaving-holding pattern of the dominant group would "elevate them (i.e., Negro slaveholders) to a position of respect and privilege."

People are what they do. John Adams of Massachusetts practiced his ethics. The second US president opposed slavery and was one of two of America's first 12 presidents who never owned people. John Adams' son, John Quincy Adams, was the other president who never owned slaves. Abigail Adams, America's first *second lady* and second *First Lady* (the latter 1797-1801), wife of a leader of the American Revolution against Britain, is reported to have used the term "evil" to characterize slavery. This advisor to America's founding presidents is said to have believed that slavery was not only evil; but "a threat to the American democratic *experiment*" (emphasis added). One story goes that in 1791 when the Adamses lived in Philadelphia, "a free black youth comes to her house and asks to be taught how to write." Abigail Adams defies her neighbors' objections and places the boy in "a local evening school." When asked to explain herself, Adams declares that "a Freeman (is) as free as any young Men." Why "is he to be denied instruction ... merely because his Face is Black?"

World Languages: US Deliberate Ignorance, Foolish Isolationism

The total number of languages in the world is reportedly "7,139." January 2020 reports by *The Intrepid Guide* list "7,117 known languages spoken by people around the world." The online encyclopedia *Info Please* lists the third most-spoken mother tongue as Hindi, and the language with the most primary language speakers as Mandarin Chinese. Recognized international languages (though lower ranked) are Arabic, Spanish,

French, and Russian. Because of the history of imperialism, the most represented languages are English, Spanish and French.[44]

An alphabetical listing of the top 20 most spoken languages are: Arabic (Standard Arabic), Bengali, Chinese (Mandarin Chinese), Chinese (Yue Chinese or Cantonese), English, French, German (Standard German), Hindi, Indonesian, Japanese, Marathi (official language, Maharashtra, India), Nigerian (Pidgin), Portuguese, Russian, Spanish, Tamil (official language of Indian state of Tamil Nadu, the sovereign nations of Sri Lanka and Singapore, and the Union Territory of Puducherry, India), Telugu (official language of Indian states of Andhra Pradesh and Telangana), Turkish, Urdu (a major language of Pakistan, India, and Nepal), Vietnamese.[45]

Considering the number of languages spoken throughout the world and the number of places where US aggression is situated, how many of these languages are taught in US schools or are enforced prerequisites for members of the US diplomatic corps? [46], [47] The most commonly taught languages in US public schools are Spanish, French, and German. Yet the United States deploys diplomatic missions in 166 of the 193 United Nations Member Nations. Included in the list are missions called "interest sections" housed in other states' embassies, in UN member states Iran and Syria; in addition to missions in Vatican City,

---

[44] "How many languages are there in the world? 7,151 languages are spoken today," Ethnologue: Languages of the world https://www.ethnologue.com/guides/how-many-languages

[45] "What are the top 200 most spoken languages?" Ethnologue: Languages of the world https://www.ethnologue.com/guides/ethnologue200

[46] "List of most commonly learned foreign languages in the United States," Wikipedia Foundation (Last modified May 30, 2022), https://en.wikipedia.org/wiki/List_of_most_commonly_learned_foreign_languages_in_the_United_States

[47] "Language education in the United States," Wikipedia Foundation (Last modified May 9, 2022), https://en.wikipedia.org/wiki/Language_education_in_the_United_States

a UN observer state; and Kosovo and Taiwan, non-member countries.[48] Though the exact total is unknown, the United States reportedly deploys hundreds of military installations and tens of thousands of military and allied personnel around the world. In addition to US presence in well-known places such as the United Kingdom and Germany, US presence in militaries and consulates also may be found in the following places (only a partial listing),[49] countries having their own distinct languages, often multiple *official* languages:

[48] "List of diplomatic missions of the United States," Wikipedia Foundation (Last modified June 20, 2022), https://en.wikipedia.org/wiki/List_of_diplomatic_missions_of_the_United_States

[49] "List of United States military bases," Wikipedia Foundation (Last modified June 23, 2022), https://en.wikipedia.org/wiki/List_of_United_States_military_bases

Afghanistan (Dari)
Bahrain (Arabic)
Bangladesh (Bengali)
Botswana (national language Tswana)
Chad (co-official language Arabic)
Croatia (Croatian)
Cyprus (Greek, Turkish)
Czech Republic (Czech)
Democratic Republic of the Congo (national languages: Kikongo, Lingala, Swahili, and Tshiluba)
Djibouti (Arabic co-official, additional Somali)
Georgia (Georgian, Ossetian, Abkhaz)
Greece (Greek)
Iceland (national language Icelandic: Islensk)
India (official language Hindi)
Iran (national language Persian: Farsi)
Iraq (Arabic)
Italy (Italian)
Jordan (Arabic)
Kenya (Swahili, English)
Kosovo Albanian (Shqip) Arbëresh, Arvanitika)

Kuwait (Arabic)
Kyrgyzstan (Kyrgyz)
Laos (Lao)
Latvia (Latvian)
Lebanon (Arabic)
Lithuania (Lithuanian)

Malta (Maltese)
Montenegro (Montenegrin)
Myanmar (official language Burmese)
Niger (Hausa, Djerma, Tamajaq, Fulfulde; official: French)
Norway (Norwegian)
Oceania (450 languages)
Oman (Arabic)
Pakistan (Balochi)
People's Republic of China (Cantonese, Chinese Mandarin)
Poland (Polish)
Portugal (Portuguese)
Qatar (Arabic)
Republic of the Congo (national languages Lingala and Kituba)
Romania (Romanian)
Russia (Russian)
Rwanda (mother tongue Kinyarwanda)
Saudi Arabia (Arabic)
Serbia (Serbian)
Singapore (official languages English, Mandarin Chinese, Malay, Tamil)
Slovakia (Slovak)
Slovenia (Slovene)
Somalia (official languages Arabic and Somali)
South Africa (official languages: Afrikaans, English, Southern Ndebele, Pedi, Sotho,

Swati, Tsonga, Tswana, Venda, Xhosa, and Zulu)
South Korea (Korean)
Sudan (official languages Arabic and English)
Syria (Arabic)
Tajikistan (Tajik)
Thailand (Thai)
Turkey (Turkish, Turkic)
Uganda (official language Swahili, most spoken Ganda)
Ukraine (Ukrainian)
United Arab Emirates (Arabic)
Uzbekistan (Uzbek)
Vietnam (Vietnamese)
Yemen (Arabic)
Zambia (mostly widely spoken Nyanja).

DR. CAROLYN LADELLE BENNETT

As Americans offer the youth dead languages and narrow sectarian languages, as leaders persist in backwardness and chaos among themselves and in US relations with other countries, the world chooses multilateralism and multilingualism, mutual respect. The world moves on, together; *and* with the best interests of their individual citizenry at heart.

The United States and its K-12 educational institutions have demonstrated a longstanding failure of national commitment to foreign language studies and investment. Long before the pandemic, which has become the easy blame for every flaw in governance, America's schools were unprepared, substantively (as opposed to militarily and commercially), for a globalized world.

More than forty states of the United States and the District of Columbia had been unable to find "certified foreign language instructors." Rural America suffers most. Not only in languages (even the chosen languages of Spanish and French); but in the fields of special education, mathematics, and physical sciences, US schools have been unable to meet staffing needs.

Across the United States, there are glaring shortcomings in "critical-need" languages such as Arabic. Studies have found that "nearly 110,000 students" in US classrooms report Arabic as their "home language." Arabic is the second most-spoken home language among English-language learners in US public schools, kindergarten through 12th grade; and Arabic is the least commonly taught language in US public schools. Scholars have observed that knowledge of Arabic and facility in speaking it is "crucial to national security." Yet, widespread, deliberate ignorance in this area suggests an American arrogance and contemptuousness bent on self harm later to be blamed on others.

Only eleven states require foreign language study as a prerequisite for high school graduation. According to pre-pandemic reports, New Jersey stands out as the exception where the state offers "the seal of bi-literacy—special recognition on high school diplomas for graduates who demonstrate fluency in two or more languages." More than half of New Jersey's public school students (including those in elementary and middle schools) are enrolled in world language courses.

The executive director of the American Council on the Teaching of Foreign Languages has raised the alarm that the future of America "depends on the ability to engage with the rest of the world." Sadly, director Marty Abbott said, "Americans have a very tough time doing that."

There is an extremist defect in character and approach that hollows out the heart of America, leaving the country and its people weakened and backward, lagging behind as the world moves on. Americans' strange relationship with language is a huge loss to America and the world.

As with the universal language (music), universal respect for spoken languages of the world and for the language of one's homeland engenders self respect and serves global understanding. Learning languages benefits self and global society: humankind.

Americans' serious study and proper use of the standard (English, American English) language of their homeland would discipline and sharpen the mind, bring clarity and cleanness to thought processes. Studying languages of other lands and cultures would help in comprehending and properly applying meanings, usage and grammatical structures of the English language—*no need to resort to profanities, insult or broken speech patterns*. The language is rich with clean choices.

Learners of languages obtain broadly useful, transferrable skills for work, profession, and community. Learning languages offers choices in work, and aids national and global mobility. Consider all those countries and moving populations whose commonly spoken language (native tongue) is Arabic or Hindi or Farsi or Dari or Vietnamese or Swahili or Portuguese or Cantonese or Uzbek or Tamil or Hausa or Russian or Shqip or Somali. Studying languages of many lands and cultures expands the mind, develops genuine respectfulness and unprejudiced appreciation for and understanding of world peoples and cultures.

If their minds (and hearts) are opened in this way, ordinary Americans will be able to overcome their susceptibility to public officials and major media's destructive propaganda, fear mongering, isolationism, and profit-making aggression. Their studied embrace of languages at home and abroad will engender thoughts of peace among themselves and peace among all peoples and nations. A patriot— not merely a dogmatist, but *one who truly cares about his homeland*—is capable of appreciating and respecting homelands of the world's peoples.

3

Part 2 Anarchism

World, Domestic News Evidence of a Strange Relationship with Language

A COMPLEX PATTERN OF aggression has been set in successive US congresses and administrations. The pattern of violence is copied on streets of America. Public officials and their industrial partners in media and elsewhere, their collective backbiting, bickering, and blame slinging, their relentless violent aggression at home and abroad has disastrous and everlasting consequences all round.

Domestic Hostility: Fighting Language

Smock, Ray. "Incivility and Dysfunction in Congress is a National Crisis." *History News Network* https://historynewsnetwork.org/article/142484#

Ray Smock is director of the Robert C. Byrd Center for Legislative Studies at Shepherd University. He served as Historian of the US House of Representatives from 1983 to 1995.

Sullivan, Andy. "'This clown' — 'Nothing smart about you': Un-presidential insults fly in first Trump-Biden debate." Reuters. September 30, 2020. https://www.reuters.com/article/us-usa-election-debate-insults/this-clown-nothing-smart-about-you-un-presidential-insults-fly-in-first-trump-biden-debate-idUSKBN26L0R8.

Curley, Grace. "Joe Biden insulting Americans with low-quality lies," *Boston Herald*. July 3, 2021. https://www.bostonherald.com/2021/07/03/curley-joe-biden-insulting-americans-with-low-quality-lies/

Collinson, Stephen. "Insults fly as Biden locks horns with Russia and China." "Chinese calls US 'condescending' in its tone in high-level meeting" *CNN* March 19, 2021. https://www.cnn.com/2021/03/19/politics/president-joe-biden-russia-china/index.html

"Pelosi boots two Republicans off Capitol Hill riot committee, GOP responds by pulling out of 'sham' investigation altogether" RT news, July 21, 2021 https://www.rt.com/usa/529869-pelosi-boots-republicans-capitol-riot/

Behrmann, Savannah. "What is going on with Rep. Marjorie Taylor Greene? Here is what happened this week." *USA Today*. May 14, 2021.[50] https://www.usatoday.com/story/news/politics/2021/05/14/rep-marjorie-taylor-greene-here-what-happened-week/5095632001/

Roebuck, Jeremy. "A Pa. high school cheerleader's profane Snapchat rant didn't warrant suspension, Supreme Court rules" *Philadelphia Inquirer News*. June 23, 2021 https://www.inquirer.com/news/scotus-mahanoy-school-cheerleader-snapchat-brandi-levy-20210623.html

---

[50] GREENE, Marjorie Taylor," Biographical Directory of the United States Congress: a Representative from Georgia; born in Milledgeville, Baldwin County, Georgia; graduated from South Forsyth High School (Cumming, Georgia, 1992); Bachelor of Business Administration (University of Georgia, Athens, Georgia, 1996); business owner; elected to the One Hundred Seventeenth Congress (January 3, 2021–term ending January 3, 2023). https://bioguide.congress.gov/search/bio/G000596 "Marjorie Taylor Greene": work experience includes "co-owning a construction company, Taylor Commercial; and owning a CrossFit gym," Ballotpedia, https://ballotpedia.org/Marjorie_Taylor_Greene "Marjorie Taylor Greene," Wikipedia Foundation, updated July 1, 2022, https://en.wikipedia.org/wiki/Marjorie_Taylor_Greene

Supreme Court of the United States "20-255 MAHANOY AREA SCHOOLS V. B.L. DECISION BELOW: 964 F.3d 170; CERT. GRANTED 1/8/2021; Lower Court Case Number: 19-1842

Question Presented: "Whether *Tinker v. Des Moines Independent Community School District*, 393 US 503 (1969), which holds that public school officials may regulate speech that would materially and substantially disrupt the work and discipline of the school, applies to student speech that occurs off campus." https://www. supremecourt.gov/qp/20-00255qp.pdf

Supreme Court of the United States June 23, 2021 [B.L. (who, together with her parents, is a respondent in this case) was a student at Mahanoy Area High School, a public school in Mahanoy City, Pennsylvania] "Supreme Court of the United States No. 20–255 *Mahanoy Area School District, Petitioner v. B. L., a Minor*, by and through her Father, Lawrence Levy; and her Mother, Betty Lou Levy. On Writ of Certiorari to the United States Court Of Appeals for the Third Circuit https:// www.supremecourt.gov/opinions/20pdf/20-255_g3bi. pdf

SCOTUS Majority affirming Third Circuit ruling: "Although we do not agree with the reasoning of the Third Circuit's panel majority ..., we ... agree that the school violated B. L.'s First Amendment rights."

Justice for the Majority (excerpt): "A public high school student used, and transmitted to her 'Snapchat' friends, vulgar language and gestures criticizing both the school and the school's cheerleading team. The student's speech took place outside of school hours and away from the school's campus. In response, the school suspended the student for a year from the cheerleading team. We must decide whether the Court of Appeals for the Third Circuit correctly held that the school's decision violated the First Amendment."

Dissenting Justice: "Perhaps there are good constitutional reasons to depart from the historical rule; and perhaps this Court and lower courts will identify and explain these reasons in the future. But because the Court does not do so today, and because it reaches the wrong result under the appropriate historical test, I respectfully dissent."

Goodin, Emily. "Nancy Pelosi calls armed Republican members of Congress 'the enemy within' and accuses them of threatening Democrats as lawmakers demand more cash for security." *Daily Mail UK*. January 28, 2021. https://www.dailymail.co.uk/news/article-9197533/Terrified-members-Congress-demand-funds-hire-24-hour-armed-guards-homes.html

Rep. Marjorie Taylor Greene is under fire for social media posts, including one where she indicates support for executing Pelosi, and for a video that shows her harassing Parkland survivor and gun control activist David Hogg.

GOP Rep. Andy Harris is being investigated for trying to bring gun onto House floor and GOP Rep. Lauren Boebert also wants to carry a firearm.

Stone, Daniel and Miranda Green. "Congressional Name-Calling, Incivility on the Rise: Death of Manners? Character attacks and biting language have increased on Capitol Hill." *The Daily Beast*.

July 13, 2017. https://www.thedailybeast.com/congressional-name-calling-incivility-on-the-rise.

Cathey, Libby and Sasha Pezenik. "'You don't know what you're talking about,' Fauci told the Kentucky Republican." ABC News. July 20, 2021. https://abcnews.go.com/Politics/fauci-rand-paul-shouting-match-wuhan-lab-research/story?id=78946568.

Collins, Eliza. "A comprehensive guide to all the insults Trump, Clinton exchanged this week."
USA Today. August 26, 2016. https://www.usatoday.com/story/news/politics/onpolitics/2016/08/26/donald-trump-hillary-clinton-insults/89406256/.

Cummings, William. "Trump slams 'low IQ' Rep. Maxine Waters who called for harassment of White House officials." USA Today. June 25, 2018. https://www.usatoday.com/story/news/politics/onpolitics/2018/06/25/maxine-waters-trump-exchange/732505002/.

"You're doing it WRONG! White House Covid-19 spokesman yells at media for quoting CDC documents on Delta variant." RT news. July 31, 2021 https://www.rt.com/usa/530753-white-house-cdc-guidelines-confusion/

Bradner, Eric, Sarah Mucha and Arlette Saenz. "Joe Biden says voters 'ain't black' if they support Trump." "Biden: 'If you have a problem figuring out whether you're for me or Trump, then you ain't black." CNN. May 22, 2020. https://www.cnn.com/2020/05/22/politics/biden-charlamagne-tha-god-you-aint-black/index.html

"Guidance to help newsrooms more accurately and critically cover issues related to Israel and Palestine." Arab and Middle Eastern Journalists Association (AMEJA). May 31, 2021. https://www.ameja.org/

4

Beyond the Beltway

News and Views Washington Needs to Hear and Heed

"THE WORLD IS a ghetto," the songwriter writes. Whether the isolation is a calculatedly segregated community or a US contrived transnational blockade, the world has descended into a ghetto—apart, armed, and fanatically afraid. Constructive change that is beneficial to the whole world needs to come, and many international sources have put forward some important ideas in this regard. Perhaps future US leaders will appreciate and heed the wisdom of other nations and leaders—civilizations, many of them, that have survived for thousands of years.

FROM WORLD ENTITIES, LEADERS, PEOPLES

Americans to the South on US Policy, Migration

US foreign and trade policies have exacerbated dangerous conditions in Central American countries and caused desperation among people in their homeland. "The answer is not more militarization of US borders or callous treatment of refugee children," says an AFL-CIO report but, rather, "a re-imagined approach to relations" in the Americas.

People pouring out of their homelands are not on leisure vacations or searching for high living, waste, and debt. They are fleeing for their lives. As with Africans and Western Asians who risk the Mediterranean

Sea on rickety boats, their lands have been torn apart by US aggression. Central American and Caribbean children and their families have long risked harsh conditions. They have traveled thousands of miles to escape unendurable conditions of "crime, violence, crushing poverty, and failed governance." En route, many of these displaced populations have been preyed upon by human traffickers, sexual abusers, and a variety of criminals and exploiters. Yet they have made the perilous journey because staying in their homeland was *not an option*.

The 2013 AFL CIO report concluded that forced migration is a problem created in part by US policies. The solution, the report said, is not walls and rhetoric; but substantive and sustained corrections and redirection of US foreign and trade policies "to focus on job creation, decent work and meaningful protection of labor and human rights." Such changes will reduce "the 'push factors' that breed desperation and displacement."[51]

Eight years after the labor report, a new (?) administration in Washington announced that the vice president would investigate underlying causes of Central American migration. It never happened. Their apparent *underlying* intent was to preserve the status quo: take the easier course, carry on as usual. At the time, Suyapa Villeda and Miguel Tinker Salas commented on the calculated ignorance and insult of the new administration in Washington. In a 2021 *Jacobin Magazine* article, they decried US Vice President Kamala Harris's performance in Guatemala telling "would-be migrants 'not to come'" to the United States—instead of acting in good faith (with courage and honesty) and acknowledging that US "imperialist meddling in Central America [had driven] millions to flee to the United States." Central America does not need "more covert action and coups," the authors counseled; and they do not need "more intervention in elections or support for narco-dictators

---

[51] "Examining the Root Causes of the Central American Refugee Crisis," AFL-CIO Reports, March 20, 2013, https://aflcio.org/reports/examining-root-causes-central-american-refugee-crisis
www.aflcio.org

or militarized drug wars."[52] Also from Cuba (as from Syria) came the sustained affirmation of its *right to be*, on its own terms. *Granma* reported on "Valuable discussions in the provinces of Ciego de Avila and Camagüey," as part of visits by the Communist Party of Cuba's Central Committee Secretariat. "Sovereignty, self-determination and independence are not on the table," *Granma* proclaimed. [53],[54],[55]

Chinese on US Unilateralism

During the summer of 2021, with the world still in the midst of a health crisis, the president of China, Xi Jinping, warned of unilateralism camouflaged as multilateralism and urged world nations to oppose "hegemony and power politics." Speaking via video feed before the seventy-sixth session of the United Nations General Assembly on September 21, 2021, President Xi Jinping set out what should be nations' top priorities. He urged "cooperation on poverty alleviation" and "food security," "COVID-19 response and vaccines," and accelerated "implementation of the UN 2030 Agenda for Sustainable Development."

As of 2022, the bloated United Nations based in the United States, Switzerland, and elsewhere had spent 30 years building on, *presumably*, good intentions. The journey has taken them from the "Agenda 21" poverty reduction plan in 1992 in Rio to the "Millennium Development

---

[52] Suyapa G. Portillo Villeda and Miguel Tinker Salas, "The Root Cause of Central American Migration Is US Imperialism," Jacobin Magazine, June 8, 2021, https://jacobinmag.com/2021/06/kamala-harris-central-america-guatemala-visit-us-imperialism

[53] "Sovereignty, self-determination and independence are not on the table." Granma national news staff, June 11, 2021, http://en.granma.cu/cuba/2021-06-11/sovereignty-self-determination-and-independence-are-not-on-the-table

[54] Gladys Leydis and Ramos López, "We defend the Revolution, above all else," Granma news, July 12, 2021, http://en.granma.cu/cuba/2021-07-12/we-defend-the-revolution-above-all-else

[55] Granma was founded October 3, 1965, "an important date in Cuban history," and is the "official voice of the Communist Party of Cuba Central Committee" https://en.granma.cu/quienes-somos

Goals" of 2000 and 2002 discussed in Johannesburg and New York City, respectively; to the 2012 assembly, again in Rio, billed "The Future We Want" that promised to enter a process of developing "Sustainable Development Goals" (SDGs) *to build on the previous Millennium Development Goals (MDGs).* Through the years, 2013 through 2022, the UN has assembled, published reports; developed a presence on social media; and declared "Commemoration Days." Seventeen SDGs are listed on several United Nations websites. [56],[57] Included in the lists are the following:

---

[56] "Do you know all 17 SDGs?" United Nations Department of Economic and Social Affairs Sustainable Development, https://sdgs.un.org/goals

[57] "2030 Agenda for Sustainable Development" United Nations High Commissioner for Refugees: The UN refugee Agency. United Nations High Commissioner for Refugees (UNHCR) headquarters Geneva, Switzerland https://www.unhcr.org/2030-agenda-for-sustainable-development.html?msclkid=059816afb10e11ec8a3084e2f445c178

Goal 1
End poverty in all its forms everywhere.

Goal 2
End hunger, achieve food security and improved nutrition and promote sustainable agriculture.

Goal 3
Ensure healthy lives and promote well-being for all at all ages.

Goal 4
Ensure inclusive and equitable quality education and promote lifelong learning opportunities for all.

Goal 5
Achieve gender equality and empower all women and girls.

Goal 6
Ensure availability and sustainable management of water and sanitation for all.

Goal 7
Ensure access to affordable, reliable, sustainable and modern energy for all.

Goal 8
Promote sustained, inclusive and sustainable economic growth, full and productive employment and decent work for all.

Goal 9
Build resilient infrastructure, promote inclusive and sustainable industrialization and foster innovation.

Goal 10
Reduce inequality within and among countries.

Goal 11
Make cities and human settlements inclusive, safe, resilient and sustainable.

Goal 12
Ensure sustainable consumption and production patterns.

Goal 13
Take urgent action to combat climate change and its impacts

Goal 14
Conserve and sustainably use the oceans, seas and marine resources for sustainable development.

Goal 15
Protect, restore and promote sustainable use of terrestrial ecosystems, sustainably manage forests, combat desertification, and halt and reverse land degradation and halt biodiversity loss.

Goal 16
Promote peaceful and inclusive societies for sustainable development, provide access to justice for all and build effective, accountable and inclusive institutions at all levels.

Goal 17
Strengthen the means of implementation and revitalize the global partnership for sustainable development.

Notwithstanding the development goals' long and winding journey toward achievement, the president of China pressed truisms that have become part of the mantra of nations of the United Nations:

- "One country's success does not have to mean another country's failure. The world is big enough to accommodate common development and progress of all countries."
- "Differences and problems among countries need to be handled through dialogue and cooperation on the basis of equality and mutual respect."
- "We need to advocate peace, development, equity, justice, democracy and freedom, which are the common values of humanity; and reject the practice of forming small circles, or zero-sum games."[58],[59]

The complexities and complications of the cyber sphere (particularly its questionable use or abuse) added to and exacerbated existing conflicts among and between nations. Leaders were deeply concerned. In July of 2021, Senior Colonel Wu Qian, spokesman for China's Ministry of National Defense, affirmed his country's "cyber sovereignty and information security and social stability" and urged all nations to resist "cyber bullying." The representative pointedly urged the United States "to explain its spying operations," and to "stop creating tension and animosity in global cyberspace."[60]

---

[58] "Xi [Chinese President Xi Jinping] urges world political parties to shoulder responsibility for pursuit of people's wellbeing, progress of mankind," Xinhua News, July 7. 2021, http://www.xinhuanet.com/english/2021-07/07/c_1310046460_2.htm
[59] "Xi calls for bolstering confidence, jointly addressing global challenges at UNGA," China Daily news, Special report by Xinhua author, September 22, 2021 http://www.chinatoday.com.cn/ctenglish/2018/tpxw/202109/t20210922_800258807.html
[60] Zhang Zhihao, "US poses 'biggest threat to global cybersecurity', ministry says," China Daily, July 29, 2021, https://www.chinadaily.com.cn/a/202107/29/WS61027b2ea310efa1bd66556f.html

Iranians on US Aggression and Impunity

Like violent aggression from air, sea or land, one nation's abuse of power amounts to an act of aggression, in effect, *war*. A nation that blocks or cuts off other nations' medical essentials, their economic and financial operations, progress on their chosen issues and in their chosen areas of development is acting with deliberate malice (indeed criminal aggression) toward the world's peoples and nations. Thus, the incoming president of Iran, Seyyed Ebrahim Raisi, denounced US sanctions as America's "new way of war with the nations of the world." He said these actions constitute "crimes against humanity, especially sanctions on medicine during a pandemic."

Iranian diplomat and ambassador to the UN Majid Takht-Ravanchi (also Takht-e-Ravanchi) reinforced the words of Iran's president when he said that "endangering others' health for political purposes is not only illegal; it is also a war crime and a crime against humanity that has to be dealt an international response. We bear a moral responsibility to stand up to sanctions, and call for their immediate removal."[61],[62],[63]

Turkish on US (Western) Ethnocentrism

The president of Turkey, Recep Tayyip Erdoğan, spoke in the fall of 2021 of the extremism and self-designated impunity of post–World War II nations. "The world is bigger than five," President Erdoğan

---

[61] "Sanctions are 'US way of war,'" President Seyyed Ebrahim Raisi of Iran addresses the general debate of the UN General Assembly's 76th session, UN Affairs, UNTV, September 21, 2021, https://news.un.org/en/story/2021/09/1100572

[62] "United States Sanctions are Crimes against Humanity," Press TV, June 3, 2021, https://www.presstv.com/Detail/2021/06/03/658205/Iran-United-States-sanctions-crimes-against-humanity-war-crimes-United-Nations-envoy-Takht-Ravanchi

[63] "World must hold US to account for supporting Daesh, new terrorism: President Raisi" [President of the Islamic Republic of Iran Sayyid Ebrahim Raisolsadati (Ebrahim Raisi)], Press TV news, September 5, 2021, https://www.presstv.ir/Detail/2021/09/05/665904/Raeisi-Macron-Iran-Afghanistan-Lebanon-US-Daesh-JCPOA-terrorism

said. The global security architecture has changed; and the "fate of humanity should not be left to the mercy of a handful of countries that won World War II."[64]

The president was speaking of the United Nations Security Council, comprised of five permanent members who also hold the veto exclusively: the People's Republic of China, the French Republic, the Russian Federation, the United Kingdom of Great Britain and Northern Ireland, and the United States of America. Though the United Nations as a whole is comprised of 193 sovereign states, with equal representation in the UN General Assembly, the hard power, the wielders of global power and suppressors of world development progress are those five countries who have maintained the status quo since October 24, 1945.

In his discussion with the press, President Erdogan had mentioned the disparaging term "Orientalism" in rejecting its use relative to Africans as well as Asians. There is relevancy in the current context of Americans' extremism: *infantilism*.

A dangerously debilitating element loosed upon the world is a cabal comprised, incestuously, of US mass media (print and broadcast press, on and offline content caves, book publishing- entertainment-reviewer enterprise), private corporate and profiteering nonprofit industrial complexes—all intertwined with ideologues, panderers and propagandists seated in and revolving in and out of government, spreading delusions variously articulated as manifest destiny, righteous cowboys v. unrighteous redskins (white hat over black hat), yes West/ no East: *all theirs / yours nil* (zero, nothing).

---

[64] "Erdogan: Turkey rejects Orientalist approach towards African continent...," (news accessed at) TRT World, October 18, 2021, https://www.trtworld.com/africa/ erdogan-turkey-rejects-orientalist-approach-towards-african-continent-50838)

John Staughton[65], an author and editor, explains "Orientalism" whose root is Orient. "Orientalism" means the East. Its opposite, "Occident," means the West. "Occident," he writes, is perceived as "the *normal* part of the world": "the center of importance," "boasting civilization" and a single "god." The "Orient" is perceived or contrived as *other*: "deviant from the norms of civilized society, where multiple gods were regularly worshipped." This willfully ignorant, centuries-old mindset, a position of *otherness* harbored by the West toward the East, "has made it easy to dehumanize Middle Eastern and Asian populations." It is a prejudice that showed itself in the "statistical reporting of casualties in Vietnam and Cambodia, Russia and Serbia"; and, in recent decades, in the reporting of "conflicts in Iraq, Afghanistan, Yemen, Libya and Syria."

For all people, it is important to be aware of the persistent delusion of Eastern inferiority-Western superiority, Staughton concludes. Understanding the concept of Orientalism and "being aware of the many ways in which it can arise" might enable people to "move through the world as free citizens of the world—*not bound by tribal prejudice or fear of the unknown*"[66] (emphasis added).

Russians on US Separatism regarding Cyber crime, Cyber security

Perhaps it is part of the West v. East syndrome that Americans (egged on by public officials and media) have a rabid reaction to a person about whom they are totally ignorant. A brief biographical note on Russian president Vladimir Putin might be instructive. He is the son of a carriage works employee and a mother who cared. He is a native of Leningrad (current Saint Petersburg) who completed his early schooling

[65] John Staughton, "Orientalism: Definition, History, Explanation, Examples and Criticism," Science ABC, November 13, 2021, updated January 22, 2022, https://www.scienceabc.com/social-science/what-is-orientalism.html?msclkid=69722406b12111ec98d7631b42813067

[66] John Staughton profiles as a traveling writer, editor, publisher, and photographer.

in that city. He studied at a "chemistry-focused magnet school under the aegis of a technology institute." Putin then studied law and completed his law degree in 1975 (in the 1990s, he completed his doctorate) at Leningrad State University after which he studied at "KGB School No. 1" in Moscow *(a law degree was a prerequisite for intelligence work)*. After graduation and an assignment to security work, he was appointed to the "Directorate secretariat," then to the counterintelligence division, and after six months, he received operations personnel retraining courses.

In the 1980s into 1990, Putin studied at the Andropov Red Banner Institute in Moscow, was trained for work in Germany; and between 1985 and 1990, he worked in East Germany and served at the local intelligence office in Dresden, during which period he earned the military rank of lieutenant colonel and was promoted to senior assistant to the agency's department head. At the end of the 1980s, he was awarded the bronze medal issued in the German Democratic Republic "for Faithful Service to the National People's Army." On his return to Leningrad in 1990, Putin became an assistant to the rector of Leningrad State University in charge of international relations (and worked on his PhD studies). June 1991, he began work as Chairman of the Committee for International Relations at the Saint Petersburg City Hall; and from 1994, concurrently, he held the position of Deputy Chairman of the Saint Petersburg City government (on starting this work, he resigned his KGB position).

In the 1990s, Putin moved into higher governmental positions:

- Deputy chief of the Presidential Property Management Directorate (1996, when he moved his family to Moscow);
- Deputy chief of staff of the Presidential Executive Office and chief of Main Control Directorate (1997, at the same time, he defended his doctoral thesis on economics at the Saint Petersburg State Mining Institute);
- First deputy chief of staff of the Presidential Executive Office (May 1998);

- Director of the Federal Security Service (July); and
- Secretary of the Security Council of the Russian Federation (from March 1999).
- Prime minister of the Russian government (August 1999) and acting president of the Russian Federation (December 31, 1999).

In the 2000s, Vladimir Putin was elected president of Russia (March 26, 2000), reelected to a second term (March 14, 2004), appointed prime minister by Presidential Executive Order (May 8, 2008). He has been proposed as a candidate for president of the Russian Federation (November 2011); and assumed office on May 12, 2012. In March 18, 2018, President Putin was reelected to the office of President of the Russian Federation.[67]

In the year Vladimir Putin was born the United States National Security Agency (NSA, successor of the US Armed Forces Security Agency) was formed as an intelligence entity under the US Department of Defense (War Department). The budget (classified) was estimated at $10.8 billion. Headquartered in Fort Meade, Maryland, the NSA operates "alongside the Central Intelligence Agency" (CIA). It maintains a physical presence throughout the world. The CIA-NSA team is "a highly classified intelligence team" that has been known to "insert eavesdropping devices in 'high value targets' such as presidential palaces or embassies. The tactics of their joint "Special Collection Service" (SCS) are said to include "close surveillance," "burglary," "wiretapping," and "breaking and entering."[68],[69]

The KGB was the main security agency for the Soviet Union (March 13, 1954-December 3, 1991), a military service governed by army laws

---

[67] "Vladimir Putin Biography" Kremlin, http://en.putin.kremlin.ru/bio/page-0

[68] "National Security Agency (NSA)," Wikipedia Foundation, updated June 29, 2022, https://en.wikipedia.org/wiki/National_Security_Agency

[69] "Generating foreign intelligence insights," "Applying cybersecurity expertise," "Securing the future," National Security Agency/Central Security Service," United States Government, https://www.nsa.gov/

and regulations. Successors in Russia to the KGB were "the Foreign Intelligence Service" (SVR) and "the Federal Security Service" (FSB).[70] The Russian Federation website describes the Federal Security Service (FSB)[71] (whose activity is overseen by the President of the Russian Federation) as "a federal executive body with the authority to implement government policy in the national security of the Russian Federation, counterterrorism, protection and defense of the state border of the Russian Federation, the protection of internal sea waters, the territorial sea, the exclusive economic zone, the continental shelf and their natural resources, ensuring the information security of Russia and exercising the basic functions of the federal security services specified in the Russian legislation…." The Russian government http://government.ru/en/department/113/

Leadership of the Russian Federation, in like manner as leadership of the People's Republic of China, implored US leadership to cooperate with world nations. At the International Cybersecurity Congress in 2018, President Putin urged: "We know very well that cyber threats have reached a scale where they can be dealt with only through the joint efforts of the entire international community." The International Cybersecurity Congress is an intersectional platform that convenes and enables global cybersecurity dialogue against the backdrop of globalization and digitalization. The Russian president emphasized the importance of world nations' developing "common rules of the game and binding international standards" that, "as much as possible," would take into "account rights and interests of all countries," and would be universally "acceptable to all." He pointed out that the "egoism and self-centered policies" of some countries were "damaging the international information stability."

---

[70] "KGB," Wikipedia Foundation, updated June 29, 2022, https://en.wikipedia.org/wiki/KGB?msclkid=d5e927cbb12911ec9439d260922797c6
[71] "Federal Security Service," The Russian government, http://government.ru/en/department/113/

Three years later, the Russian Federation continued to urge cooperation from the United States of America. Foreign Minister Sergey Lavrov called for "productive dialogue on cyber security issues." He said the Russian Federation was "actively working on adopting a code of responsible behavior of states in the global information space, given the interests of each country in the field of military and political security." They were "promoting the project of a universal convention on combating cyber crimes."[72]

UN Human Rights Chief on High-tech Surveillance Abuses by States and Criminal Gangs

United Nations member states also were concerned about cyberspace and related security. The head of the United Nations Office for Disarmament Affairs, Izumi Nakamitsu, in 2021 sounded the alarm about the blame fest and its consequences. He cautioned about individual "states' adopting offensive measures for technology uses that are considered hostile" together with "armed (non-state) criminal groups' developing potentially destabilizing capabilities, with a high degree of impunity."[73]

The United Nations Office of High Commissioner for Human Rights, headed by Michelle Bachelet, observed that aggression against journalists and human rights defenders (e.g., arrests, intimidation, assassination) had been tied to surveillance software. Commissioner Bachelet urged governments to "take immediate steps to end human rights-violating uses of surveillance technologies; and to institute regulatory apparatuses that curb the distribution, use and export of surveillance technology."[74],[75]

---

[72] "Russia seeks productive dialogue with US on cyber security—Lavrov," TASS News Agency, June 24, 2021, https://tass.com/politics/1306651

[73] "'Remain vigilant' against malicious technologies that could imperil future generations," UN news, June 29, 2021, https://news.un.org/en/story/2021/06/1094992

[74] "Pegasus: Human rights-compliant laws needed to regulate spyware," UN news, July 19, 2021, https://news.un.org/en/story/2021/07/1096142

[75] Verónica Michelle Bachelet Jeria is a native of Santiago, who took her medical degree at the University of Chile. She is a physician and politician who served Chile

From World Press Corps (news and opinion)

The News and views from across the world were often quite different from the narratives emanating from within the Washington (DC) Beltway.

"China slams US for thwarting UN meetings on Palestine-Israel issue." Xinhua. May 14, 2021. http://www.xinhuanet.com/english/2021-05/14/c_139946206.htm

"US brings nothing but poverty, backwardness to nations across globe: IRGC chief commander." Press TV news. July 26, 2021. https://www.presstv.ir/Detail/2021/07/26/663087/Salami-IRGC-Iran-US-maximum-pressure-sanctions-backwardness-

"Iran: Global conscience awakened to apartheid Israel's barbarism." Press TV May 18, 2021. https://www.presstv.com/Detail/2021/05/18/656927/Iran-Rabiei-Israel-Palestine-Gaza

"We're told US's only option is to escalate aggression against Russia & China: the statement is untrue; dé·tente (relaxation of strained relations or tensions between the US and these nations) IS possible" by Caitlin Johnstone, RT opinion. May 5, 2021. https://www.rt.com/op-ed/522979-aggression-russia-china-detente/

---

as its thirty-second and thirty-fourth president (2006–2010; 2014–2018). She is multilingual. In addition to Spanish, Bachelet is fluent in English, German, French, and Portuguese. Before assuming the Chilean presidency, Michelle Bachelet was minister of health and minister of national defense (2000–2002 and 2002–2004, respectively). During separate presidential terms, she was president pro tempore of the Union of South American Nations (UNASUR) from 2008 until 2009; and president pro tempore of Pacific Alliance, the Latin American trade coalition, from 2016 until 2017. Between presidential terms, she was Executive Director of United Nations Women (2010–2013). On September 1, 2018, she became United Nations High Commissioner for Human Rights.

"(The United States) is whipping up fear of China because Washington simply cannot contemplate a world it does not dominate" by Tom Fowdy, RT opinion. April 16, 2021. https://www.rt.com/op-ed/521257-us-china-whipping-up-fear/

"Palestinian women lead resistance against Israeli occupation." Turkish Press (Anadolu Agency). May 16, 2021. https://turkishpress.com/palestinian-women-lead-resistance-against-israeli-occupation/

"Turkey reiterates call on Israel to end attacks on Palestinians." Turkish Press. May 10, 2021. https://turkishpress.com/turkey-reiterates-call-on-israel-to-end-attacks-on-palestinians/

"'Turkey will forever stand by Palestinians in their fight for freedom'" Turkish Press. May 15, 2021. https://turkishpress.com/turkey-will-forever-stand-by-palestinians-in-their-fight-for-freedom/

"World community for love of humanity, to stop brutality against Palestinians." Iran Press. May 17, 2021. https://iranpress.com/content/39555/world-community-for-love-humanity-stop-brutality-against-palestinians

"Liberals demanding pro-Western policies from Moscow simply 'don't understand Russian genetic code'—" Foreign Minister Lavrov claims." RT news April 28, 2021. https://www.rt.com/russia/522345-lavrov-liberals-understand-genetic-code/

"Overwhelming majority of Russians believe Crimea is legally part of country, including those who don't support Putin, poll reveals" by Jonny Tickle. RT news. April 28, 2021. https://www.rt.com/russia/522325-majority-crimea-part-poll/

> The vast majority of Russians (86 percent) support
> Moscow's re-absorption of Crimea, with most convinced
> that the country did not violate international obligations

and agreements when it gained control of the Black Sea peninsula in 2014.

"'Poisoned by politics': The WHO's [World Health Organization] emergencies chief calls for end to 'disturbing' discourse around probe into pandemic origins." RT news. May 28, 2021. https://www.rt.com/news/525120-who-pandemic-origins-probe-poisoned-politics/

"Propaganda Scrambles Our Minds: Notes from the Edge of the Narrative Matrix" by Caitlin Johnstone. September 17, 2021. https://caitlinjohnstone.com/2021/09/17/propaganda-scrambles-our-minds-notes-from-the-edge-of-the-narrative-matrix/

"Afghanistan: Same, Same; Again, Again" by Armstrong, Patrick. Strategic Culture Foundation." September 1, 2021. https://www.strategic-culture.org/news/2021/09/01/afghanistan-same-same-again-again/

"It is no longer 1992. Somebody call the US and tell her that" by Sieff, Martin: "The World Transformed and No One in America Noticed." *Russia Insider.* June 26, 2018. https://russia-insider.com/en/politics/world-transformed-and-no-one-america-noticed/ri23930

Twenty years from September 11, 2001, amid protracted, extreme aggression by the United States, one writer wonders *What if* another path had been chosen.[76] *What if* another set of priorities had been implemented? What could the dead have done with their lives? What is knowable is that "$5.8 trillion" (of waste, fraud, abuse, rabid aggression) could have helped *establish justice* and *ensure domestic tranquility, provide for the common defense* and *promote the general welfare* and, within society, *secure freedom* and independence for current and future generations. The writer lists the loss and what might have been.

---

[76] "Two decades on from 9/11, the US has paid a heavy price for its War on Terror," RT news, September 11, 2021, https://www.rt.com/usa/534360-war-on-terror-cost-americans/

- $5.8 trillion could have funded veterans' benefits and services for twenty-six years.
- $5.8 trillion could have covered Social Security for five years, with enough money left over to send every American man, woman, and child an $800 stimulus check.
- $4.5 trillion could have converted the United States to an entirely renewable energy grid.
- $2.6 trillion could have completed modernization of America's aging infrastructure.
- $5.8 trillion could have covered SpaceX CEO Elon Musk's folly (*not my choice*) of "colonizing Mars and making humans an interplanetary species."

"From Glorious Millennia to Death and Destruction: Zionists Rewrite Palestine's Story" by Miko Peled. Mint Press news, analysis. September 20, 2021. https://www.mintpressnews.com/glorious-millennia-death-destruction-zionist-rewrites-history-of-palestine/278495/

"Iran highlights US rights violations on 'American Human Rights Week'" by Yusef Jalali. Press TV news. June 26, 2021, https://www.presstv.ir/Detail/2021/06/26/660926/Iran-US-human-rights-violation-crimes-

"Washington mobilizing, commanding al-Qaeda, Daesh terrorists in Bayda Province: Yemen." Press TV news. July 7, 2021. https://www.presstv.ir/Detail/2021/07/07/661688/Washington-supporting-and-mobilizing-al-Qaeda-Daesh-terrorists-in-al-Bayda-Yemeni-minister

"US sanctions Cuban police force as Biden threatens more penalties during meeting with Diaspora group leaders." RT news. July 30, 2021. https://www.rt.com/usa/530754-us-sanctions-cuban-police/

"Partnership good for peace across Asia" by Martin Sieff. *China Daily* opinion. July 19, 2021. https://www.chinadaily.com.cn/a/202107/19/WS60f4b2c5a310efa1bd662a63.html

"'CPEC bringing socio-economic development for Pakistan': official."
Xinhua news Interview. July 17, 2021. http://www.xinhuanet.com/
english/2021-07/17/c_1310066422.htm

"US will be disappointed forcing SE Asian countries to get on its anti-
China chariot" by Mu Lu.
Global Times opinion July 29, 2021. https://www.globaltimes.cn/
page/202107/1230031.shtml

"Southerners were 'the first victims' of American imperialism and
have been 'slandered,' claim the Sons of Confederate Veterans"
by Chris Sweeney. RT news June 5, 2021. https://www.rt.com/
usa/525709-sons-confederate-veterans-slandered/

North Americans and Russians reportedly labeled this
Anachronism

The North Atlantic Treaty Organization or North Atlantic Alliance is
a Cold War era Washington-originating West against East global war
machine (1949 – present) that US presidential candidate Donald Trump
called "obsolete and extremely expensive to the United States."[77] In a
2017 exchange with the press, US President Donald Trump referred to
his earlier comment, saying, "'I said it was obsolete.... 'We must not be
trapped by the tired thinking that so many have, but (must) apply new
solutions to face new circumstances throughout the world.'"[78]

---

[77] "Would a Trump America walk away from NATO? The US has long warned
its European partners it was losing patience with paying the majority of NATO's
bills. The nomination of Donald Trump has made the threats of a US withdrawal
from NATO seem real and present," Deutsche Welle August 15, 2016, https://www.
dw.com/en/would-a-trump-america-walk-away-from-nato/a-19475314
[78] "Trump says NATO is 'no longer obsolete': US President Donald Trump
urged 'new solutions to new circumstances' for the alliance after meeting NATO
Secretary-General Jens Stoltenberg," DW April 12, 2017 https://www.dw.com/en/
trump-says-nato-is-no-longer-obsolete/a-38407650

"Although NATO has been justifying its measures to overhaul its military potential by the need to counter threats on all fronts," said Russian diplomat and deputy minister of Foreign Affairs, Alexander Viktorovich Grushko, "we cannot help noticing that all these efforts are focused on countering Russia." In the years 2012 through 2018, Grushko was the permanent representative of Russia to NATO.[79]

Writer and former diplomat Patrick Armstrong said in an interview with Sputnik news, "NATO is incompetent, incapable of operations against any but the defenseless…. Its main goals are self-perpetuation and validation of arms sales."[80]

The North Atlantic Treaty Organization (OTAN or NATO) has an expense account estimated in 2019 at $1.036 trillion. Its leadership is dominated by a Supreme Allied Commander (Europe), a position held by United States Air Force General Tod D. Wolters until July 4, 2022, when US Army General Christopher G. Cavoli assumed the command.[81],[82]

---

[79] "NATO 'Deluded' Policies Pose Dangers to Europe, World Peace." Sputnik News, November 14, 2017, https://sputniknews.com/20171114/nato-new-military-command-structure-1059071466.html

[80] Patrick Armstrong is a former analyst with Canada's Department of National Defense specializing in the USSR/Russia (1984) and former counselor with the Canadian embassy in Moscow (1993–1996). His current writings with the organization Katehon focus on Russia and related subjects. On its website, Katehon is described as a think tank "engaged in studying 'great spaces' comprised of "the majority of all world civilizations" (North America, South or Latin America, Europe, Russia-Eurasia, China, India, the Islamic world, Africa, and the Pacific)—"global-regional 'poles'" that possess "commonalities and differences which should be neither ignored nor denied;" but rather embraced as "a new multipolar approach to studying each civilization, and the many subtle distinctions that exist within them."

[81] "NATO," https://www.nato.int/cps/en/natohq/index.htm
"NATO Secretary General at Allied Command Operations change of command," North Atlantic Treaty Organization Press Release, July 4, 2022, https://www.nato.int/cps/en/natohq/news_197705.htm?selectedLocale=en&mode=pressrelease

[82] "NATO," Wikipedia Foundation updated July 2, 2022, https://en.wikipedia.org/wiki/NATO

From Global Thinkers Past and Present
Basic Principles Mindful of Future Generations

United States officials concerned with their own private interests—not even the genuine interests of the United States of America—seem determined to dilute, diminish and utterly destroy the founding principles and motivations of the United Nations. The attack must end and the abuse must be prosecuted so that all peoples are ensured protection (security) in their homelands; and the sovereignty of individual nations is preserved, without prejudice or foreign interference. Vital institutions and international agreements established following early and middle twentieth century wars and war crimes are essential in contemporary times. The Charter of the United Nations is among those essential documents. Among the aims of the 1945 Charter are these.

- Saving succeeding generations from the scourge of war, "which twice in our lifetime has brought untold sorrow to mankind"
- Reaffirming faith in "fundamental human rights, in the dignity and worth of the human person, in the equal rights of men and women and of nations large and small"
- Establishing "conditions under which justice and respect for the obligations arising from treaties and other sources of international law can be maintained"
- Promoting "social progress and better standards of life in larger freedom.[83]

In an effort to counter the rabid self-serving order of contemporary times, representatives of some nations have spoken out boldly and taken courageous nonviolent action to urge the return of the principled order, honor and good intentions. Without threatening or harming the United States of America, many apparently well-intentioned groups, nations and leaders have attempted to capture and retain peacefulness and

---

[83] United Nations Charter (full text), United Nations, https://www.un.org/en/about-us/un-charter/full-text

DR. CAROLYN LADELLE BENNETT

nonviolence, and preserve nuclear nonproliferation. These nations also were concerned with protecting their own sovereignty from chronic and criminal US aggression.

One group calls itself "Group of Friends in Defense of the Charter of the United Nations." Its Member States include some of the same nations that endorsed the Universal Declaration of Human Rights, proving that true progress, constructive progress is taking the best from the past, expanding it, making it more inclusive, and making it better. Nations listed among the Group of Friends in Defense of the UN Charter are these.

Algeria	Iran
Angola	Laos
Belarus	Nicaragua
Bolivia	North Korea
Cambodia	Palestine
China	Russia
Cuba	Saint Vincent and the Grenadines
Equatorial Guinea	Syria
Eritrea	Venezuela

In March of 2021, the Group of Friends pointed to conditions that, for a long time, have presented a clear and present danger to the whole world. Some of the conditions and reckless behavior cited by the nations were: the increasing resort to unilateralism marked by isolationist and arbitrary actions, the imposition of unilateral coercive measures; the cavalier withdrawal from landmark agreements and multilateral institutions; and the attempts to undermine critical efforts of nations to attend to common concerns and global challenges.

The United Nations established in the early postwar period (October 24, 1945) had laudable aims of saving future generations "from the scourge of war;" "reaffirming faith in fundamental human rights;" "establishing conditions under which justice and respect for the obligations arising from treaties and other sources of international law could be maintained," and "promoting social progress and better standards of living *in larger freedom*" (emphasis added). Nowhere in the UN Charter was there a declaration of—or commitment to—unending brutality (*humanitarian massacre*) by external or transnational forces holding the biggest arsenals of lethal weaponry; no pledge of constant destabilization and bombing of nations or egging on conflicts or instilling division, or pervasively, relentlessly and quixotically, even schizophrenically undermining one or another nation's sovereignty, its domestic culture, leadership, or manner of being.

The Group of Friends in Defense of the Charter of the United Nations urged dialogue, tolerance, and solidarity. They emphasized the timelessness of the original basic principles enshrined in the Charter— as opposed to the contemporary abuse and misuse of them by bullies and cowards. The early principles and actions, they said, are "the core of international relations," and they "remain vital for peaceful coexistence among nations." From its standpoint, the organization pledged to work toward preserving, promoting and defending "the prevalence and validity of the UN Charter," and, at the same time "providing a platform for promoting the prevalence *of legality over force*" (emphasis added)[84],[85],[86]

[84] United Nations: UN Web TV, "Virtual Launch of the Group of Friends in Defense of the Charter of the United Nations," July 6, 2021, https://media.un.org/en/asset/k1w/k1w1qatav5

[85] Joselyn Ariza MFA Venezuela, "Launch: 'Group of Friends in Defense of The United Nations Charter,'" Popular Resistance, July 9, 2021, https://popularresistance.org/launch-of-the-group-of-friends-in-defense-of-the-charter-of-the-united-nations/

[86] "Group of Friends in Defense of the Charter of the United Nations," Wikipedia Foundation (updated April 6, 2022), https://en.wikipedia.org/wiki/Group_of_Friends_in_Defense_of_the_Charter_of_the_United_Nations

Eliminate Nuclear Weapons

The Republic of Ireland's former president, a distinguished jurist and former United Nations High Commissioner for Human Rights was alarmed in 2019 that relations between the two major nuclear powers (the United States of America and the Russian Federation) were "at a worryingly low ebb, shrouded in mistrust and confusion" and lacking any "constructive dialogue on the subject" of nuclear weapons. Mary Robinson recalled that people growing up "in the era of US-Soviet confrontation took the (nuclear) threat seriously ...." However, in the post-USSR period, "a dangerous complacency" has set in, as if "nuclear weapons were somehow 'old news.'..." She cautioned of this "grave mistake," given that "the risk of nuclear war is higher (now) than at any time since the end of the Cold War."

What is required, Robinson insisted, is that nations recommit "to the values of multilateralism that underpin the United Nations" so that current generations may "bequeath to future generations a peaceful, livable world."[87], [88] Earlier leaders seemed to have understood that mutual obliteration is not a sane course, and if set in motion, neither side (no one) would be there to claim *victory*. Even an American B-film actor turned US president was aware of this, as recalled by a Russian leader.

---

[87] Mary Robinson, "Nuclear weapons are still the greatest threat to world peace. NATO must take action now to protect humanity," The Independent-UK, December 3, 2019, https://www.independent.co.uk/voices/nuclear-weapons-threat-nato-summit-trump-leaders-new-arms-race-a9230546.html. The Elders, "Nuclear weapons are still the greatest threat to world peace. NATO must take action now to protect humanity," Mary Robinson on Nuclear Disarmament, December 3, 2019, https://theelders.org/news/nuclear-weapons-are-still-greatest-threat-world-peace-nato-must-take-action-now-protect

Mary Robinson of Ireland was an academic, barrister, member of the Irish Senate (1969–1989); president of the Republic of Ireland (1990–1997); and United Nations High Commissioner for Human Rights (1997–2002). Currently, she chairs the Elders, which is described on their website as "an independent group of global leaders working together for peace, justice and human rights."

[88] "Who we are: an independent group of global leaders working together for peace, justice and human rights," The Elders, https://theelders.org/who-we-are

The Soviet leader who may be credited, at least in large part, with building the bridge between eastern and western Europe and transitioning from the Union of Soviet Socialist Republics (including the Russian Soviet Federative Socialist Republic) to the Commonwealth of Independent States (Armenia, Azerbaijan, Belarus, Kazakhstan, Kyrgyzstan, Moldova, Russia, Tajikistan, Uzbekistan), and the Russian Federation is Mikhail Sergeyevich Gorbachev.

This son of Russian-Ukrainian peasants and of a father who had been wounded while serving in the Russian Army when the Nazis invaded the USSR[89] was the eighth and final leader (1990–1991) of the USSR. In 2021, Mikhail Gorbachev reflected on new thinking that has arisen since that earlier era and recalled important discussions with US President Ronald Reagan—discussions in which the two leaders declared that "nuclear war must never be fought." Therefore, "the ultimate goal is nothing short of the elimination of nuclear weapons."

In the final analysis, Gorbachev wrote in an August 2021 opinion piece, "No challenge or threat facing humankind in the twenty-first century can have a military solution," and "No major problem can be solved single-handedly by one country or even a group of countries." At the heart of this new thinking is "the proposition that humankind's common interests and universal human values must be the overarching priority in an increasingly integrated, interdependent world," Gorbachev said. And while national interests, class, corporate or other interests are not to be denied or negated, the new thinking places front and center "the interest of saving humanity from the threat of nuclear war and environmental catastrophe."[90]

---

[89] "Mikhail Gorbachev," Biography: The Arena Group, https://www.biography.com/political-figure/mikhail-gorbachev

[90] Mikhail S. Gorbachev, "Perestroika and New Thinking: A Retrospective," Global Affairs, August 9, 2021 (an article in translation of text by the author in the Russian language previously published in *Global Affairs*, https://globalaffairs.ru/articles/ponyat-perestrojku/ https://eng.globalaffairs.ru/articles/perestroika-and-new-thinking/

The American writer and speaker Helen Adams Keller wrote, "Every great movement passes through four stages." First, men ignore it. Then they ridicule it. Later they persecute it. Finally, she wrote, "they raise monuments to it."[91] In contemporary times, "anti-militarists may seem unpatriotic, disloyal." But in the course of time, men and majorities will come to realize "that the true security of nations lies in *subordinating interests of clan* and country to a worldwide love of man, and *service from all to all*" (emphasis added).

One of America's old and distinguished soldiers declared as an enduring imperative: disarmament with mutual honor and confidence. Looking into the distant future and seeing a world growing ever smaller, US President Dwight David Eisenhower cautioned in his final message to the nation that Americans "must avoid becoming a community of dreadful fear and hate." And instead must be "a proud Union of mutual trust and respect."[92]

End US-Supported Terrorism

The call for peace and the end of US global violence has come from global and domestic leaders. At least two US elected officials have authored legislation aimed at ending the post-911 hemorrhaging of war funding, the justification for waste, and the unending aggression. Former Congresswoman Tulsi Gabbard of Hawaii in 2017 sponsored

---

[91] Keller, Helen, "A Protest against Militarism," speech 1916, American Foundation for the Blind, Helen Keller Archive, Series 2: Writing about/by Helen Keller, Box 212 Speeches:1903 – 1932, Folder 3 speeches: 1916-1917, https://www.afb.org/HelenKellerArchive?a=d&d=A-HK02-B212-F03-006&e=-------en-20--1--txt--------2-7-6-5-3--------------0-1

[92] Dwight D. Eisenhower, "Farewell Address," January 17, 1961, in American Rhetoric, (authenticity certified, text version transcribed directly from audio Audio mp3 of the address) https://www.americanrhetoric.com/speeches/dwightdeisenhowerfarewell.html

the "Stop Arming Terrorists Act" (H.R.608)[93] that would prohibit the use of federal agency funds to provide assistance to Al Qaeda, Jabhat Fateh al-Sham, the Islamic State of Iraq and the Levant (ISIL), or any individual or group that was affiliated with, associated with, cooperating with, or adherents to such groups. The bill also would have prohibited federal agency funds to any foreign government found by the US Office of the Director of National Intelligence (ODNI) to have assisted the identified category of groups or individuals within the most recent 12-month period.[94] The bill had fourteen cosponsors who were Members of the House in 2017: Representatives Peter Welch of Vermont, Thomas Massie of Kentucky, Barbara Lee of California, Walter B. Jones Jr. of North Carolina, Thomas A. Garrett Jr. of Virginia, Ted S. Yoho of Florida, Paul A. Gosar of Arizona, Scott Perry of Pennsylvania, John Conyers Jr. of Michigan, Dana Rohrabacher of California, Ro Khanna of California, Bobby L. Rush of Illinois, Jeff Duncan of South Carolina, and Peter A. DeFazio of Oregon.

In a C-Span video in December of 2016, Representative Gabbard had urged passage of the bill. She pointed out that US "taxpayer dollars

---

[93] "H.R.608: Stop Arming Terrorists Act," 115th Congress (2017-2018), Library of Congress, https://www.congress.gov/bill/115th-congress/house-bill/608; https://www.congress.gov/bill/115th-congress/house-bill/608/all-info

[94] Tulsi Gabbard is an American soldier and public official, a native of Leloaloa of American Samoa; from age 2, Hawaii. Her resume includes service in US military (an officer serving with Hawaii Army National Guard, 2003, in Iraq, 2004–2005 with the Medical Company, Twenty-Ninth Support Battalion, Twenty-Ninth Infantry Brigade Combat Team, Logistical Support Area Anaconda, with Twenty-Ninth Brigade Special Troops Battalion, Twenty-Ninth Infantry Brigade Combat Team of the Hawaii Army National Guard (posted to Kuwait.2008–2009); with the Hawaii Army National Guard, the 351st Civil Affairs Command, and the United States Army Civil Affairs and Psychological Operations, 2020). She was a member of the Hawaii House of Representatives (December 2002–December 2004); a Member of the Honolulu City Council (January 2, 2011–August 16, 2012); and member of the US House of Representatives (January 3, 2013–January 3, 2021). Her academic credentials came from Hawaii Pacific University with a concentration in international business; Alabama Military Academy officer training school. Her military rank is major.

are being used to strengthen the very terrorist groups we should be focused on defeating." This fact, she said, "should alarm every Member of Congress and every American." Instead of spending "trillions of dollars on regime change wars in the Middle East," the Congresswoman said, "we should be focused on defeating terrorist groups like ISIS and al-Qaeda, and using our resources to invest in rebuilding our communities here at home." After Gabbard's formal introduction of the bill on January 23, 2017, it languished and died in the Foreign Affairs and Intelligence committees.

In March of 2017, Senator Rand Paul[95] of Kentucky introduced a companion bill in the US Senate: S.532 (Stop Arming Terrorists Act)[96] and not a single senator joined him as cosponsors. The bill was read twice and died in the Committee on Foreign Relations. After sponsoring the bill, Senator Paul said in a public statement that there is within the United States government a strain of "addiction to war and colonization" that has caused "never-ending conflict throughout the world; and, in more recent years, the emergence of radical terrorist groups like al-Qaeda and ISIS." The senator observed that although political leaders "have been known to verbalize the need to fight terrorist groups …; in reality, their policies, in many cases, have been to arm and support them."[97]

---

[95] Randal Howard Paul is an American physician and public official, native of Pittsburgh, Pennsylvania, reared in Texas; from age thirty, the State of Kentucky. He has served in the United States Senate since January 3, 2011. His academic credentials include studies at Baylor University in Texas and a medical degree from Duke University Medical School in North Carolina.

[96] "S.532: "Stop Arming Terrorists Act," 115th Congress (2017–2018) introduced in Senate (03/06/2017) … prohibits the use of federal agency funds to provide covered assistance … https://www.congress.gov/bill/115th-congress/senate-bill/532

[97] Huff, Ethan, "Rand Paul introduces 'Stop Arming Terrorists Act,'" Rand Paul news, March 22, 2017. https://www.randpaul.news/2017-03-22-rand-paul-introduces-stop-arming-terrorists-act.html

End Killing by Remote Control

Ban Killer Drones[98] is an organization formed by a group of US-based writers and activists who make up "an international grassroots campaign committed to banning aerial weaponized drones." The group argues that the problem with these instruments is their utter detachment from shared humanity, community, and civilized existence. The video game–like operation of drones allows not only deniability and the labeling of criminal behavior as *other than* criminal; it confers on both giver and taker of orders (heads of state, military officers or sinister contractors and executioners, operators or *gamers*) a sense of *godly consciencelessness.*[99]

The manmade callousness of *unmanned* aerial vehicles perpetrates, provokes, and propagates violent aggression without cause or offense. The sinister nature of weaponized drones, enabling remote killing, prompts and encourages perpetrators of these operations—whether by act near or far, by order, legislation, policy or acquiescence—to take military action that would have been impossible or impermissible had they attempted to deploy traditional military personnel on the ground (up close) in the presence of their victims. Yemen is but the latest (at the time of this writing) and most horrifying *detached* manmade crisis. Political and military conditions have been inflamed and civil conflict deepened and prolonged spilling over into "a regional war with ghastly impact on the lives of hundreds of thousands of people."

US leaders of the past had authorized the United States as signatory to important international human rights and statutory documents. However, contemporary US leaders have breached post–World War II and later international conventions and principles with

---

[98] The Ban Killer Drones website lists their key figures as Chelsea Faria, Kathy Kelly, Nick Mottern, David Swanson, and Brian Terrell, https://bankillerdrones.org/
[99] Ban Killer Drones, "Dangers: Section 2. Weaponized Drones–Unprecedented power to kill and traumatize with minimal or no consequence to the perpetrator" (paper, 2020), https://bankillerdrones.org/dangers/

flagrant impunity. The Ban Killer Drones documentation mentions particularly the text of articles 1–3, 5, 7, 12, and 20 of the 1948 Universal Declaration of Human Rights (UDHR). They cite these articles to highlight the violations inherent in the use of weaponized drones. Signatories of the UDHR endorsed the principles that all human beings are born free and equal in dignity and rights; and as they are endowed with reason and conscience, they should act toward one another in the spirit of brotherhood: fraternity, society, fellowship. No distinction or superficiality should deny or prevent the treatment of human beings as equals. By virtue of their humanity, all human beings have the right to life, liberty, and security of their person. As human beings, all should be free from torture, cruel, inhuman, or degrading treatment or punishment; granted due process under law; the right to privacy; and freedom to peacefully assemble and associate.

The Ban Killer Drones activists conclude their article with a kind of warning that human beings always have choices, and choices have consequences. In this context, the critical choices are "whether to use death-dealing weapons" and "which weapons to use." The future of individuals, of societies, and "of humanity itself" rests on decisions taken by men (human beings).

The document that became the Universal Declaration of Human Rights was first raised at the 1946 (first) session of the United Nations General Assembly. In February 1947, the original drafters of the International Bill of Human Rights were (alphabetically)

- Chinese academic, philosopher, playwright, and diplomat Peng Chun Chang (P. C. Chang);
- Lebanese philosopher and diplomat Charles Habib Malik; and
- American writer, diplomat, and social and political activist (former United States First Lady) Anna Eleanor Roosevelt (Eleanor Roosevelt).

The drafters were assisted by the United Nations Secretariat and UN Human Rights Division director, a Canadian lawyer, diplomat, and scholar, John Thomas Peters Humphrey. He was tasked with creating a preliminary draft. From March 27, 1947, the drafting committee was made up of members of the Commission on Human Rights for Australia, Chile, China, France, Lebanon, the Union of Soviet Socialist Republics, the United Kingdom, and the United States.[100], [101], [102], [103], [104]

Fifty-eight member countries of the United Nations were present at the December 10, 1948, assembly considering the Universal Declaration of Human Rights. Forty-eight countries voted yes.

[100] "Peng Chun Chang," Wikipedia Foundation (updated August 29, 2015), https://infogalactic.com/info/Peng_Chun_Chang?msclkid=f64e12b2b2aa11ec9d2236b8c7718ab6

[101] "Charles Malik," Infogalactic (updated January 9, 2016), https://infogalactic.com/info/Charles_Malik

[102] "Eleanor Roosevelt," Infogalactic (updated May 30, 2016), https://infogalactic.com/info/Eleanor_Roosevelt

[103] William Edward Kaplan and Laura Neilson Bonikowsky "John Humphrey," The Canadian Encyclopedia, March 16, 2011 (Updated by Andrew McIntosh, February 4, 2022), ttps://www.thecanadianencyclopedia.ca/en/article/john-peters-humphrey?msclkid=09eab853b2ac11ec8af73c8fe0182ee5

[104] "Universal Declaration of Human Rights: Drafters of the Declaration," United Nations, February 1947 drafters Eleanor Roosevelt, Pen-Chun Chang and Charles Malik; Director of the UN Secretariat's Division for Human Rights, John Humphrey, https://www.un.org/en/about-us/udhr/drafters-of-the-declaration

1. Afghanistan	17. Egypt	33. New Zealand
2. Argentina	18. El Salvador	34. Nicaragua
3. Australia	19. Ethiopia	35. Norway
4. Belgium	20. France	36. Pakistan
5. Bolivia	21. Greece	37. Panama
6. Brazil	22. Guatemala	38. Paraguay
7. Burma	23. Haiti	39. Peru
8. Canada	24. Iceland	40. Philippines
9. Chile	25. India	41. Siam
10. China	26. Iran	42. Sweden
11. Colombia	27. Iraq	43. Syria
12. Costa Rica	28. Lebanon	44. Turkey
13. Cuba	29. Liberia	45. United Kingdom
14. Denmark	30. Luxembourg	46. United States
15. Dominican Republic	31. Mexico	47. Uruguay
16. Ecuador	32. Netherlands	48. Venezuela

Eight countries abstained.

1. Byelorussian Socialist Soviet Republic (SSR)	4. Saudi Arabia	7. United Socialist Soviet Republic (USSR)
2. Czechoslovakia	5. Ukrainian Socialist Soviet Republic (SSR)	8. Yugoslavia
3. Poland	6. Union of South Africa	

Two countries (Honduras and Yemen) did not vote either yes or no.[105],[106],[107],[108]

"Patriotism" without Zealotry, Extremism

Helen Adams Keller was enlightened and in the early twentieth century she enlightened others about patriotism. "Children everywhere must learn that true patriotism is a sense of responsibility for the welfare of one's fellows," she wrote. It involves one's "desire to do something to enrich the life of the community." The young must be introduced to "heroes in the work for peace." They must be taught that "heroism for peace is the highest courage." Educational institutions must impress upon young and impressionable minds "that peace and goodwill" among nations are essential conditions for progress.

Communities within the United States of America are much healthier when individuals focus their efforts on mending relations with fellow Americans and avoid the easy course of teaching America's young and impressionable to fear and view as enemies the children and youth of

---

[105] "International Bill of Human Rights: Universal Declaration of Human Rights" Resolution adopted by the United Nations General Assembly, Vote Summary: 48 yes; 8 Abstentions; 2 Not voting (yea or nay), December 10, 1948, Dag Hammarskjold Library, UN Human Rights Documentation United Nations Digital Library, https://digitallibrary.un.org/record/670964?ln=en

[106] "Universal Declaration of Human Rights" (full text), United Nations (Paris, December 10, 1948, General Assembly resolution 217 A) https://www.un.org/en/about-us/universal-declaration-of-human-rights?msclkid=06073dc2b2a611ec9069b1095daa914e

[107] "International Relations," Universal Declaration of Human Rights (UDHR), November 15, 2021 https://theinternationalrelations.com/universal-declaration-of-human-rights-udhr/#:~:text=The%20document%20which%20later%20become,the%20General%20Assembly%20in%201946.?msclkid=46acbac0b2b011ec89163b1f66d895b9

[108] "Universal Declaration of Human Rights," Wikipedia Foundation (updated June 21, 2022), https://en.wikipedia.org/wiki/Universal_Declaration_of_Human_Rights?msclkid=62f16dd5b2a711eca5aa3d330382f39c

DR. CAROLYN LADELLE BENNETT

other countries and cultures. Keller argued against throwing up the hands with an easy helplessness: "men have always fought and will always fight." The position is fallacious, a distraction perpetrated by men and women who profit from war and conflict. The truth is, Keller wrote, that peoples of many nations have the power (and her conviction still holds among many people whose voices never make the news pages or websites of major media) "to bring about permanent peace and universal goodwill." Her advice in 1931 remains sound. Forget the "fear and hate" of the past. Begin, in the present moment, to "build powerful public opinion against war" (hostility, aggression). "Prepare ..., with all our might, to live peaceably among the peoples of the earth."[109] Helen Keller was one of those courageous American women born in the nineteenth century. She was a prolific author and pubic speaker, a world traveler, and a tireless campaigner for peace.[110]

Since "god" is a subjective or tribal notion and therefore a divisive one, its use is out of place in one people's affirmation of patriotism or allegiance to the Union—the United States of America, one shared state and nation. A critical flaw in the American character is feigned patriotism camouflaging an incestuous and rabid self-indulgence. The most overt show in this blemish is the display of tattered American flags ringing car dealerships, hanging over endless eateries, flapping from big motorized vehicles, or lining major thoroughfares. If asked to recite the American Pledge of Allegiance, the owners, managers, and pseudo patriots, would be at a loss. So here is an insidious progression from an envisaged perfect *Union* to the panderers' tribal *extremism*.

---

[109] Helen Keller. "Our Great Responsibility," Helen Keller Archive, American Foundation for the Blind, Speeches: 1903 – 1932: "Helen Keller's speech advocating for world peace over war" 1931, https://www.afb.org/ HelenKellerArchive?a=d&d=A-HK02-B212-F10-009
[110] Helen Keller was born (June 27, 1880) in America's Deep South and died (June 1, 1968) in New England. She holds a place in the Alabama Women's Hall of Fame (1971) and in the Alabama Writers Hall of Fame (2015).

- American Pledge of Allegiance (1892): "I pledge allegiance to my Flag and the Republic for which it stands, one nation, indivisible, with liberty and justice for all."

- American Pledge of Allegiance (1923–1924): "I pledge allegiance to my Flag and to the Republic for which it stands, one nation, indivisible, with liberty and justice for all."

- American Pledge of Allegiance (1924–1954): "I pledge allegiance to the Flag of the United States and to the Republic for which it stands, one nation, indivisible, with liberty and justice for all." This is my choice.

- American Pledge of Allegiance (1954–present *4 USC §4*): "I pledge allegiance to the Flag of the United States of America, and to the Republic for which it stands, one Nation under God, indivisible, with liberty and justice for all."

The issue is clearly controversial but it is my view that the insertion of deity, no doubt in a moment of political pandering, is a divisive element that breaches the essential rule of keeping separate the government (matters of state) *of*, *by*, and *for* all the people (as one)—from individually subjective preferences, such as religion (faith, creed). To proclaim and uphold a government rule that prohibits discrimination against those who hold or espouse a creed, cult, or doctrine is a separate and distinct rule. This rule should be maintained. However, to effectively endorse, promote, or demand that all citizens adopt or pledge their allegiance to such a creed, cult, or doctrine is quite another issue; and this practice should be outlawed. The insertion of "god" into the American pledge of allegiance was a grave error. It carries a message that misguides, distracts, and cripples generations of American citizens because it annuls and invalidates the *Union* of the United States of America.[111]

---

[111] "The Pledge of Allegiance" (versions 1892 – present) United States Historic Documents, https://www.ushistory.org/documents/pledge.htm?vm=r

DR. CAROLYN LADELLE BENNETT

5

American Extremism
Final Words

Toward a More Perfect Union

Character of a Nation

AMERICA'S YOUNG AND impressionable are subjected to round-the-clock, unchecked, and even celebrated violence. Government officials cheer led by mass media order and legislate violence at home and abroad. Yet Americans are "shocked"—feign shock—whenever homegrown mass shootings come to American schools, theaters, and supermarkets. As gun violence spread across the nation in 2022 with several events involving mass shootings, many politicians, media personalities, social media writers and illustrators together with an array of ideologues amused themselves with *gun talk*: "who should and should not own guns;" "how and when and where and what kind of gun" should people own or not own.

The game had been lost long ago: long before the first shot was fired, long before the gun arguments (part of the guns-gays-gods circus) began. The use of lethal weaponry signifies deep and compelling loss—loss that long preceded any choice, mobilization or discharge of deadly force. Use of deadly weaponry (including the sale) signifies human failures: a carelessness that mounts over time: is cumulative, complex, and multilayered. People in institutions and communities' (including global to local governments, profit-taking and "nonprofit" or "not-for-profit" industry personnel and partners') have failed to engage respectfully, civilly, and in sustained dialogue. People in institutions and communities' (including global to local governments, profit-taking and "nonprofit" or "not-for-profit" industry personnel and partners') have failed to unearth, address, mend and solve human relations problems and issues, conditions and inadequacies in social (including work) environments; inadequacies in general institutional resources and specifically in educational, physical and mental health and recreational institutions and related spaces, cordial commons, staffing, services, and resources.

Instead of rolling up the sleeves, sitting down together, and working seriously throughout systems; instead of attending to and solving broad and deep institutional, individual and societal problems—people in power concentrate *only* on holding on to power. People in institutions and communities (including global to local governments, profit-taking and "nonprofit" or "not-for-profit" industry personnel and partners) have a penchant for political and tribal pandering, pageantry, round-the-clock distraction of the citizenry.

They create and publish slogans. They promote erecting public statues, or tearing down public statues. They support the waving of historic flags, or banning them. They declare days of remembrance—veterans' days, mental and physical illness days, human trafficking and homelessness days—accompanied by "moments of silence" and "thoughts and prayers," flag lowering and handwringing, displays of flowers and religious emblems at sites of death. *Hear them ring*: these gestures commemorating failure, and the consequences of failure.

The 2022 nationalization of "Juneteenth" was one of those pandering flights of exploitation, and regression. The act reflects equal amounts of ignorance and manipulation. Some people are dissatisfied, ignorant, stuck in a fancied past so a powerful political class of multicolored partisan profiteering panderers (at the expense of the stuck, ignorant, and angry) leap in with equal offerings of *nothingness* and *regress*. Raise a

DR. CAROLYN LADELLE BENNETT

statue or tear it down; name a street or rename a street; name or rename a day or a month; and the mental and physical gates and ghettoes remain. Potholes and litter spread. Trains and planes fail to run on time, stay in the skies, or on the rails. Bridges fall. Mothers' sons (and daughters) are indoctrinated to kill and be killed at home and abroad. Neighborliness is denied, discouraged, and nonexistent. Washington and friends' anachronistic "Juneteenth" fantasy feeds anger, cements ignorance, widens the gulf among Americans, and severs the *United States of America.*

US Violence in direct action and on orders continued in 2021 through 2022, and the costs continued to mount. According to reports by the Brown University Cost of War Project, the US post-9/11 wars have caused the displacement of least "37 million" people; and have left an estimated "30,177" US active duty personnel and veterans dead from suicide.[112],[113],[114],[115]

---

[112] "Costs of War: Human, Economic, Social and Political," https://watson.brown.edu/costsofwar/costs

[113] "New Costs of War Study: 37 Million Displaced by US Post-9/11 Wars," Costs of War Project, September 8, 2020, "In September 2020, the Costs of War project released a new report entitled, 'Creating Refugees: Displacement Caused by the US Post-9/11 Wars,' outlining the number of people displaced as a result of post-9/11 wars," Brown University Watson Institute for International and Public Affairs, https://watson.brown.edu/research/2020/Post-9/11DisplacementStudy

[114] Thomas Howard Suitt III, "High Suicide Rates among United States Service Members and Veterans of the Post-9/11 Wars, Boston University, Papers: High Suicide Rates among United States Service Members and Veterans of the Post-9/11 Wars," June 21, 2021, Costs of War, June 21, 2021, PDF: "20 Years of War: a Costs of War Research Series," Brown University Watson Institute for International and Public Affairs, https://watson.brown.edu/costsofwar/files/cow/imce/papers/2021/Suitt_Suicides_Costs%20of%20War_June%2021%202021.pdf

[115] David Vine, Cala Coffman, et.al., "Creating Refugees: Displacement Caused by the United States' Post-9/11 Wars," August 19, 2021, MAJOR FINDINGS: The US post-9/11 wars have forcibly displaced at least 38 million people in and from Afghanistan, Iraq, Pakistan, Yemen, Somalia, the Philippines, Libya, and Syria. This exceeds those displaced by every war since 1900, except World War II." PDF https://watson.brown.edu/costsofwar/files/cow/imce/papers/2021/Costs%20of%20War_Vine%20et%20al_Displacement%20Update%20August%202021.pdf

The Iraq Body Count website in 2022 documented "186,201 to 209,422" civilian deaths from violence, noting that further analysis of the WikiLeaks' Iraq War Logs estimated another "10,000 civilian deaths."[116]

Reports published by the Gun Archive website showed gun deaths within United States totaled 43,671 (mass shootings 610) in 2020. In 2021, they reported 45,010 gun deaths (mass shootings 692). By the summer of 2022 (before Independence Day), they were reporting 20,729 gun deaths (mass shootings 278). Among the dead were hundreds of children and thousands of teenagers.[117]

Americans tend to lunge from crisis to crisis, from blame fest to blame fest, from bold headline to bold headline (sprinkled with hand-wringing "shock" and "thoughts and prayers") — with no concern for or attempt to address preexisting conditions such as poverty, fear, and ignorance. Breaches in people relations persist. Community is lost. Trust between citizenry and public service or government fails. Misplaced priorities and inadequate social, economic, educational, and leisure staffing and resources mount. Incest and nepotism plant a permanent state of decline: poor work ethic, unfit intellectual and experiential quality, and incompetence, unfit moral, psychological and ethical character— disease that is insidious and malignant.

Self-reflection and forthrightness require enormous courage. It is difficult to admit without equivocation I am *whom I accuse*: I am the *extremist*.

The contemporary breed of elective officials and their incestuous partners cycling in and out of government have virtually undone the

---

[116] Iraq Body Count, latest update May 30, 2022, https://www.iraqbodycount.org/database/
https://www.iraqbodycount.org/
[117] Gun Violence Archive, 2020-June 2022, https://www.gunviolencearchive.org/past-tolls
https://www.gunviolencearchive.org/

founding principles and their potential; trivialized and invalidated the living essence of established government—*Union* in the United States of America. They have instilled unrelenting animosity among lawmakers and between legislative and executive branches of government so much so that they have made important work on behalf of the citizenry, the body politic, a lasting impossibility. In the judiciary and throughout the appointive court system, they have installed partisan-prejudiced puppets, color-coded and ideological narrow-mindedness that has diluted and made virtually impossible an essential impartiality in law, a studied objectivity, demonstrated qualification, and true honorableness. They have flaunted lawbreaking in US domestic elections and surrounding systems, including campaign financing and census taking and districting. They have legislated unlawfulness as lawfulness in a variety of government-involved venal, monetary or mercenary operations and exchanges. They have finagled contracting and installed a self-serving public-private partnering vested in undermining the legitimacy of public service. They have so impaired operations and institutions and services that nothing works as it should in America. Public officials as a class no longer work or pretend to work ethically and honorably, diligently, and efficiently, congenially, respectfully, and cooperatively. They have broken America and wrapped it in a red, white, and blue-striped death cloth.

Across the world, extending at least to the First World War era through the current post–Cold War era, US leaders and their partners have ordered, instigated or led violent aggression in Western Asia and Northern Africa. This long period of aggression has done serious harm to majority Muslim countries such as Afghanistan and Pakistan, Egypt and Turkey, Iran and Yemen, Somalia and the Sudan. The whole of the troubled area called the Middle East, though defined variously, can encompass at least twenty countries: Cyprus (non-European), Turkey, Syria, Lebanon, Israel, the West Bank and Gaza, Jordan, Iraq, Iran, Afghanistan and Pakistan, Saudi Arabia, Yemen, Oman, United Arab Emirates, Qatar, Bahrain, Kuwait, Egypt, and Libya. Most Muslims live in North and Central Africa, the Middle East, and Southeast Asia.

US leaders have flaunted lawbreaking in US transnational affairs from Iran-Contra to Guantanamo Bay to cyberspace and from regions of the Mediterranean to the Caribbean to the Caspian and Black Seas, and the Red Sea to the South China Sea.

They have threatened and imprisoned US lawyers engaged in human rights work; threatened and made direct attacks on lawyers (prosecutors) of the International Criminal Court. They have assassinated or caused to be assassinated leaders, scientists, and soldiers of other countries. They have even barred other nations' athletes from international games. Entrenched US leaders and their partners have a penchant for throwing up walls and wiles, *even wails* of distraction. And aided and abetted by technological conglomerates, mass media and entertainment industrialists, they carry on a never-ending barrage of blame against *convenient* "demons"—arbitrary *others*.

America's leaders engage in breaking countries, failing states and associates of 193 nations making up (and allied with) the United Nations. The portrait of the United States of America today under its current crop of leaders and their partners is a portrait in backwardness, barbarity (inhumanity), criminality, incestuousness, and decay. And one wonders as to the possibility of later generations' raising America from the ashes. Is it possible that America's future generations— sufficient numbers of undistracted, self-reflective, law-abiding, civic and independent-minded youth and forward-looking internationalist adults—will join in *turning the tide*?

Quality of the Future: Character of the Youth

For the past thirty years, post–Cold War era leaders of the United States of America, the French Republic, and the Kingdom of Britain and Northern Ireland have commanded vast and interminable aggression causing unpardonable devastation to majority Muslim nations. Media including entertainment media have produced, directed, funded and

DR. CAROLYN LADELLE BENNETT

cheered a notion of clashing civilizations: battles to the death. Millions of people in Western Asia and Northern Africa have been forced to flee their homelands. They have been forced into the Mediterranean. Many have been victimized by profiteering traffickers. Many have died in the crossing. On their arrival in Europe (if they manage to arrive), many have been physically abused and openly disparaged.

In this moment of man-made tragedy, without letup a schoolteacher in the French Republic chooses publicly to declare an individual "right" to insult Muslim leaders. Together and individually, these acts of extremism on the parts of "Westerners" are followed by another act of extremism manifest in a bombing incident that occurs in the French Republic.[118],[119] It is in this context that the Supreme Leader of the Islamic Republic of Iran, Sayyid Ali Hosseini Khamenei (Ayatollah Haajj Sayyid Ali Khamenei), in 2015, appealed, at least twice, to the young.

As long as "double-standards dominate" and "powerful supporters" divide "terrorism" (or terrorists) into "'good' types and 'bad' types" and as long as singular governmental interests hold sway over human and ethical values, the Supreme Leader said—"the roots of violence should not be looked for in places *other than* the West." Using words not unlike those used by the American speaker Helen Adams Keller, he

---

[118] Agence France-Presse "French police detain students after teacher's beheading," October 21, 2020. Background: 47-year-old Samuel Paty, a schoolteacher of history "had shown his pupils a cartoon of Mohammed." This teacher was later "killed outside his school in Conflans-Sainte-Honorine," a suburb of northern Paris. An alleged assailant was then killed by French police. https://www.news.com.au/world/europe/french-police-target-islamist-networks-after-teachers-beheading/news-story/b39f16ff3c024e7209fa713568404773

[119] France24, "November 2015 attacks: A timeline ..." Friday, November 13, 2015, starting at 9:16 p.m. (8:16 p.m. GMT): "Simultaneous shootings and suicide bombings take place across the centre of Paris and the suburb of Saint-Denis" (130 people died and many were injured." November 17-18, 2015: "Police raid a house in the northern suburb of Saint-Denis, where two men involved in the attacks are hidden. One of the men detonates his explosive vest," resulting in the deaths of the two men and a women. https://www.france24.com/en/france/20210908-paris-november-2015-attacks-a-timeline-of-the-night-that-shook-the-city

urged youth to search diligently for the truth: "to lay the foundation for correct and honorable interactions based on accurate understandings, deep insight, and lessons learned from horrible experiences." And with diligence and an earned confidence, contribute to the building of firm foundations "engendering security and peace;" and "bequeathing hope and a bright future that illuminates all the earth."[120],[121]

The Supreme Leader of the Islamic Republic of Iran Sayyid Ali Hosseini Khamenei (Ayatollah Haajj Sayyid Ali Khamenei) was among the founders of the Islamic Republic Party in 1979. In 1980, he became chairman of the High Council of Revolution Culture Affairs and a member of the Islamic Consultative Assembly; in 1988, president of the Expedience Council; in 1990 chairman of the Constitution Revisal Comity. In a decision taken by the Council of Experts after the death of Imam Khomeini, he became Supreme Leader of the Islamic Republic of Iran.[122],[123]

Not only is the Leader, Ayatollah Haajj Sayyid Ali Khamenei, an imam who in his youth studied with great teachers and scholars, he is also an author, lecturer, and scholar in the areas in which he was taught: jurisprudence and its principles, philosophy logic, revolutionary and

---

[120] Seyyed Ali Khamenei, "Message of ayatollah Seyyed Ali Khamenei, Leader of The Islamic Republic of Iran, … To the Youth in Europe and North America," Office of the Supreme Leader, January 21, 2015 https://www.leader.ir/en/content/12798/To-the-Youth-in-Europe-and-North-America

[121] Seyyed Ali Khamenei, Azar 8, 1394, "To all the youth in Western countries," Office of the Supreme Leader, "In his second letter to Western youth, Ayatollah Khamenei Urges Western Youth to Facilitate Correct Interaction with Muslims … 'To all the youth in Western countries'"
November 29, 2015, https://www.leader.ir/en/content/13964/Ayatollah-Khamenei-issues-a-second-letter-to-the-youth-in-Western-countries

[122] "Supreme Leader of the Islamic Republic of Iran Sayyid Ali Hosseini Khamenei," The Office of the Supreme Leader, https://www.leader.ir/en/biography

[123] The Council of Experts or Assembly of Experts "is a clerical body empowered to appoint, monitor performance, and dismiss the Leader of the Islamic Revolution," MEHR News Agency, https://en.mehrnews.com/news/170250/Leader-to-receive-Assembly-of-Experts-members

DR. CAROLYN LADELLE BENNETT

political thought. He was also a political revolutionary and soldier; survivor of many imprisonments and at least one (1982) assassination attempt.

The Supreme Leader of Iran is clearly a wise man, and one far wiser than I am. Yet while I too have hopes that the young will reflect, mend, and move forward, it seems that in and around Washington, the young are under the spell of Washington and are merely mimicking opportunists accepting the destructive ways of their elders.

It seems that once the founding era faded or was forced to fade, mercenaries and tribalist exploiters set in with a vengeance. Among the *celebrated* younger exploiters and extortionists is a man named Andrew Yang. Sadly, some Americans have taken this man seriously. Often in their desperation, Americans fall in love and become the easy prey of shysters. Like con artists of all ages, Andrew Yang calls to mind the nineteenth-century's Boss Tweed (New York's Tammany Hall). Yang is asking Americans to sell their citizenry duty to him—to relinquish for a piece of coal their constitutional right and duty to make independent choices. Give him their vote and he will order the emptying of the US treasury to pay them not to work, not to create, not to produce, not to contribute to the country. Such maneuvering reflects American politicians' contempt for the government and for the people of the United States of America.

Andrew Yang has an interesting dossier. He is a job-hopper, a dabbler who subsists on nonprofit profit taking; and, though he is in every way a failure and unqualified, substantially, for US public office, he has presumed (and been permitted) to run for the US presidency and for the mayoralty of a US global city, one of the most complex and troubled cities in the world. The Columbia University graduate's campaign promise is "free money"—not from his pocket. This is a Washington pattern taken most recently, during the pandemic by the administrations Donald Trump and Joseph Biden. Instead of using funds constructively and in the process building trust among working people; instead of equipping public institutions such as schools so that they could carry on with their work, public officials in Congress and the Executive Branch often emboldened by the courts threw (borrowed) money; invited further graft. Not only did they fail (or even attempt) to solve pressing problems—and mounting *unpreparedness*. They made matters even worse. The administration taking the helm in 2021 and proceeding through 2022 joined forces with American corporate media in replacing front-page headlines of Americans and America's suffering with twisted headlines hawking another US-led war on Russia's border (all the while setting up the target to be used in their distraction and carrying on an endless stream of invective and blame against the president of Russia).

True Progress

How can Americans return to an ideal, a prospect, promise or potential for building *a more perfect Union*? First of all, actions have to comport with words.

We are not what (or who) we say we are. *We are what we do.* People who steal are thieves and people who kill are killers. Plunderers and assassins are barbarians. The actions of American leaders, major media and a variety of partners affect not only Americans; but men, women and children, institutions, cultures, livelihoods, economics, development, wellbeing throughout the world. Therefore, leadership should walk with care and humility. Rights should not be rationale for recklessness loosed on greater society comprised of one nation or of many nations. Movement of our nation toward a more perfect Union is dependent on the quality of the nation's institutions and its leaders and the preparedness of its people. What constitutes *a more perfect Union* and what is involved in proper movement toward that end should capture the imagination and inform the efforts of all Americans.

Breach or Bridge

We are what we do, not what we say. Americans in high position and positions of inordinate influence have demonstrated to the world that, to them, *nothing is sacred*. They have violated everything from nature to common decency and common sense; violated meaning and meaningfulness. They have violated each other, violated law and language, violated peoples and nations, violated community, civility and neighborliness. And to the world they declare, "We are the *good* guys."

In its active form, breach means to break or to violate.

Bridge means to join; perhaps repair and join, or join in repairing. American leaders have done a whole lot of breaking of people, places, things, and relations; and a whole lot of violating of laws, treaties, and principled institutions. The extremist breaks and stubbornly, arrogantly refuses to bridge.

In 2020, when election results were again disputed, US leaders had an opportunity to bridge. But by that time, their actions had so deeply divided lawmakers into uncivil, factional opposites and so severely severed relations between US federal office and US municipalities (left-right-black-white-blue-red) that separate camps could only dig in on opposite sides: one side claiming flawless elections; the other side claiming fraudulent elections. This is *extremism: infantilism, nihilism, anachronism, anarchism.*

For a long time, a volcanic-like undercurrent (or an undercurrent of volcanic proportions) has been active in the United States of America. Leaders should have been aware of this and responded appropriately. They have hundreds of people working for them so there is no excuse for ignorance about the true condition of the nation and its people. When confronted with the elections crisis, despite their differences or perceived differences, federal leaders should have reached out immediately to governors and other municipal officials across party lines. In closed sessions *(technology can be put to good use)*, they should have worked together to craft an agreement ordering independent investigations of all aspects of US elections, the investigative teams and all operations to be staffed by individuals from outside US partisan and Washington circles (possibly drawing on investigatory agencies of the United Nations). In the meantime, the election results could have been allowed to stand and the transfer of government proceed as prescribed by statute. The agreed to investigations would continue independently (without insider leaks or media interference) until findings are known and published. These findings would then be used to inform necessary repairs in US elections systems, machinery, personnel, and processes. Had leaders acted honorably and intelligently on behalf of the entire country, there likely would have been no January 6, 2021, affair and no further made-for-television Capitol Hill spectacle that continued through the following year.

Extremists are cowards who refuse to admit their wrong or to mend. Americans have a whole lot of mending to do, at home and abroad.

MENDING
STRUCTURES, MINDSET, PRIORITIES, PREPAREDNESS

We are what we do. Not what we say. Not who we say we are. Not what we say we believe.

America is unprepared because its leaders are corrupt and its people are distracted. US industry does not reflect the industry and ingenuity of the Americans but rather a singular enterprise. In every major city is found the industry of destruction and waste. Variously manifested is found the buying, selling, and causing of death; the consummation and discard of tangibles and intangibles. Ordinary Americans, perhaps in search of education and a better chance, are used up in Washington inmates' foreign theaters of aggression. On return to their homeland, they are *abandoned* to the streets. Instead of creating, contracting,

DR. CAROLYN LADELLE BENNETT

deploying, and taking the money (kickbacks, bribes, also known as hefty campaign contributions) of mercenaries, American leadership should fund quality education that prepares Americans for present and future work, and invention. Build a solid multifaceted industrial base in which people can get good jobs, stable jobs, living-wage jobs, apprenticeships, growth; where workers can learn and provide a sense of solidity with useful industry.

Casual work or the side hustle is carelessness, which offers the worker no substantive preparation or work skills, no profession, or career path. As a careless pursuit, casual work lacks essential reciprocity, mutual commitment between the employing institution and the employed. It is unconcerned about the quality of effort, quality of product, or quality of service. Stable work and essential reciprocity aids industry and workers. Substantive work helps ensure healthy workers. It supports a healthy society and nation. US Federal and state governments' support of Pretoria, South Africa-born Elon Reeve Musk's hobbies (electric cars, space X) and Albuquerque, New Mexico-born Preston Jorgensen's (Jeff Bezos') worker exploitative, mass consumption/waste-promoting (box-toting) billionaire businesses effectively robs public treasuries, erodes the essential, contributive work ethic, and lowers the quality of the general society including the natural environment.

As a matter of *common defense* (not offense masquerading as "defense" or "humanitarianism" against world nations), America's leaders must actively encourage and provide for the development of a body of diverse American workers, inventors and creators, professionals, artists, crafters and technicians; not billionaires or billionaire *wannabes*. Perhaps the realization of *government of the people* and their sustained thought and diligence in these particular areas might be a starting point for forming *a more perfect Union*.

Americans must learn to be self-reflective, and honest with themselves. Instead of committing the deflective tactic of comparing or, usually ignorantly, attempting to compare or contrast other countries and peoples with the United States, Americans should examine their own past record and compare it with their present performance and results. Honest people must admit that US systems are broken. Americans are responsible for the brokenness. And, together, Americans have within their power the ability to see and set right the country's brokenness. Americans must turn off the easy road of falling in love with (i.e., pledging their allegiance to) political parties, personalities, pigmentations and clans, posh-talking Ivy Leaguers, shyster lawyers, and politicians.

Clean house: Sever Incestuous lineage

Americans must clean house in Washington. Former president Donald Trump on the campaign trail had mentioned emptying the "sewer." It is a task that is particularly difficult for distracted, lazy people. But it has to be done. The stranglehold of kleptocracy and gerontocracy, incest and nepotism, anarchy, and anachronism must be severed. The framers of the Constitution seem to have been generally opposed to political parties, and perhaps that is one way. It is certainly true that the contemporary Republican and Democratic parties' grip on power is prohibiting open debate; denying entry of different voices, varied ideas, authentic dissent, clear opposition into the public area. The present situation is in effect a singular party of global aggression which leaves the electorate without choice. America's young people who are eligible voters have seen through the sham; and have given up on the entire *undemocratic* system.

Once the housecleaning is completed and the revolving door dismantled (or as this is being done), Americans must build a new breed of men and women eligible and fit for service in public office. There should be no more illiterates or obscenities. If something is worth having, it is worth preparing oneself for. No more contenders for public office who have no prior, demonstrated commitment to governance, to the country: to the Union. Superficialities such as race, creed, color, or accidents of birth or ancestry should not be treated as qualification (because they

DR. CAROLYN LADELLE BENNETT

are not qualifications) for public office, or for any office or position. Retirement age should mean retirement; therefore, no public official's age should exceed sixty-five. Longevity is not an asset in this context. Younger people holding office should undergo in-service training or apprenticeship so that the prevailing notion—that a gerontocrat should be retained in office because he or she holds all pertinent knowledge about the workings of congressional office or more generally the branches of government and their roles—is dispelled.

Term limits should be institutionalized and enforced across the country, not only at the federal level in Washington. The situation in New York has shown, repeatedly, that family ties and open-ended tenure produce feckless, careless (often abusive), and corrupt politicians whose contagion spreads throughout public office. No governor should be allowed more than two four-year terms (eight years). No US senator should be allowed more than two six-year terms (twelve years). No US Representative should be allowed more than four two-year terms (eight years). The ending terms (eight or twelve years, further reduced if disability sets in) should end eligibility for elective office.

Remove the taint. America's public office-related processes including campaigns, districting, elections, and tenure or seating in office have been corrupted and compromised. At the national and local levels, external influences including all forms of monetary influences or gifts (real or apparent) should be removed from political campaigns and from elections or electoral operations, precincts, and persons. The machinery for casting ballots should be standardized: operated offline, *tamperproof*, verifiable, and efficient. Precinct or Election Day workers as with voter registration officers should be paid out of government's general budget; they should not be in the employ of any political party organization. Related to this is the issue of who is permitted to cast a vote for contenders for public office. Voting is the right (and duty) of citizens. The right to vote in the United States should be limited to holders of US citizenship. While eligibility to vote should not be subject to poll tests or poll tax, eligibility to vote should be verifiable.

Public office candidacy must be credentialed, honest and intelligent. Written agreements on qualifications and decorum should precede staged candidate performances. Exchanges of insults, mudslinging and grandstanding should be outlawed, strictly monitored, and penalized. During debates, candidates should be subjected to intelligent examination. They should be required to engage in civil dialogue and actual debate on serious public concerns, and national and international issues. Candidates must provide evidence of their qualifications and public record documentation of their fitness to serve. Candidates for public office at the federal level should have demonstrated knowledge of world and US history, politics, and current events (not mere prejudices and talking points). Candidates or potential contenders for local and state office also should have demonstrated substantive knowledge, skills, and abilities directly pertaining to the office for which they are contending.

Debate organizing, oversight, referee, and questioning positions and panels should be independent of partisan participation and influence. Members of the questioning panel should have demonstrated professionalism, not merely connections to sources of power and influence.

Venal influences or the appearance of these should be outlawed. Public office related activities should be monitored, the rules enforced and infractions prosecuted. People and public office (even those who subject candidates to examination during candidates' debates) should not be purchasable. If someone wants to buy public office or a candidate for public office, let him or her move to a country where slavery is legal, where corruption is endorsed, and where people are bought and sold like meat.

DR. CAROLYN LADELLE BENNETT

Public Sector: Public Good

The government (public)-private intrigues and partnerships should be abolished. The revolving door should be dismantled. The bribery chain (or appearance of same) between government officials and nongovernmental or profiteering entities (including religious, quasi-religious, "nonprofit" entities) should be broken. If personnel of the Centers for Disease Control or Institutes of Health, Education or Welfare, for example, want to enter the private sector, let them do so before entering government. If they are hired by the US government, they should be required to break all ties with private enterprise and maintain clean and clear allegiance to America's Republic. Upon leaving government, they should be required to maintain several years' separation from private matters bearing on their public service employment. It is untrue that the best qualified people are in industry. If the professional corps of the US government is weak, it is because infiltrating private interests, and government-entrenched gerontocrats and kleptocrats have weakened it, deliberately.

All matters of religion and religious agency should be removed from institutions and affairs of state. This is not a criticism of the character of other nations nor is it a criticism of religion; but, rather, a strict reading of the character (the *Union*) of America. Individuals and groups seeking to interchange or supplant the American character with their own subjective beliefs (private, political, or ideological interests) have abused, misused, and purposely misinterpreted the character of America. In their quest for godly dominion, they set out to impose their interests and beliefs on an entire nation. Like private capitalism, sectarianism is a private matter and private concern; not a public matter of public concern. Therefore, Catholic, Protestant, Jewish, and other agencies, "charities" political action committees should be required to stay within the bounds of their own groups; and, under enforced law, should be prohibited from influencing or in any way participating in or interfering with the government of the United States of America.

The firm separation of "Church and State" should be resurrected and strictly enforced.

Establish public financing and end private financing of political campaigns. End slavery once and for all time. Break the dependency of private enterprise on government financing and public officials' dependency on the bribery chain: quid pro quo. Corruption is corruption. Conflicts of interests are just that, whether apparent or real. A duck walks like a duck. *We are what we do.* If public officials want to get rich, fine; let them get rich by the sweat of their own brow, and somewhere other than in and around government of by and for the people of the United States. If private enterprise wants to do business in America, they must expect rules, abide by rules, and submit to statutory oversight and regulatory demands of government of by and for the people of the United States. No threats of taking business to other countries, off shoring services, employing cheap labor, and returning cheap products and services to the United States. The return of products and services should be met with strict inspections, tough and rigidly enforced tariffs. No free lunches for the people. No free lunches for businesses or nonprofit profiteers.

Establish living-wage work not homelessness as a right. It is not enough to say "shelter" under the 1948 Universal Declaration of Human Rights is a "human right" because US officials have habitually ignored all established treaties of peace and human rights (preferring only pervasive aggression treaties manifest in such entities as NATO). Home ownership is not the issue. The issue is basic, permanent shelter. *A tent is not shelter.* A camp is not a home in American society. Like casual work, homelessness reflects the character of American officials who callously discard Americans in the same way that they discard "allies," and manufacture "enemies." The inhumanity of this leaves one at a loss for words.

Build a functioning common defense corps whose focus of work is America's preparedness, a corps that is subjected to regular examination and required, regularly, to show hard evidence of achievement of predetermined goals. The problem with various US "independent" governmental or nongovernmental "improvement" entities is that they improve nothing. They are handed funds and left to their own self-perpetuating devices. Quality teaching and learning are part of the common defense of America and it cannot be left to self-perpetuating entities.

Quality Schooling

America needs schoolteachers (good teachers, qualified teachers, standard English-speaking teachers) in basic fields (reading, writing, arithmetic, Standard English, health and sciences, ethics). America needs good teachers in technology, trades, music, arts and crafts; and qualified teachers in a broad array of spoken languages, histories and cultures of world countries. This will expand learning for its own sake and learning for global understanding. Such advancement in the knowledge and skills repertoire of American children and youth will provide them with great opportunities and options for all kinds of work at home and abroad. America needs properly trained and ethical doctors, nurses, and related medical professionals, as well as research scientists. Americans must reduce and even erase the country's state of unpreparedness.

Therefore, public officials must redirect government funding from agents and contractors of aggression to builders and rebuilders of appropriate agencies tasked with ensuring (and monitoring the funding for) the education and reeducation, training and retraining, development, and deploying of an essential (active and reserve) work corps of Americans. This support and funding should be earmarked and reflective of substantive, life-affirming, all-round values—neither tribal nor reflective of trends, trivialities, individual or ideological predilections or fancies.

As a matter of set law (not political pandering or whimsy), Americans should redefine, clarify, and reassert the terms *common defense* and *general welfare*. As a matter of principle based on observation, I do not believe in "free" education for Americans because the culture of the United States is not suited for that model. I do believe in strictly monitored support in critical fields for the overall strengthening of the nation. On many levels over many years, the process of "financial aid" has been abused and misused and broken down from its original intent (as intimated in Madison in the 1700s and later expressed in the Morrill Act of 1862 (Land-Grant College) supported by Abraham Lincoln and congressional colleagues led by Justin Morrill). Often higher education upper-level personnel have squandered federal funding. Many have used funds to copy trends such as expanding institutions beyond their mission and capability; to ingrain nepotism and cronyism ensuring lowered standards and reductions in the quality of faculties and administrations; and often out-and-out theft, diverting federal funds to private use and personal extravagance.

Intermingling of college funding and private corporate banking should be eliminated. The private sector and public sector have different goals, reasons to be; and they should be kept separate and distinct (just as matters of state and sect should be kept separate). College staffs of all kinds should be carefully monitored, penalized, and permanently barred from participation in college funding (or student financial aid programs) if graft (illicit gain) is discovered during regulatory oversight. For many years, top officials in American colleges and universities have been abusing the system, destroying colleges, and students' opportunities *(I have observed this firsthand).*

While there have been loud complaints about the high cost of student loans, less attention has been paid to corruption in the system of financial aid perpetrated by higher education officials, lending establishments, and lax or nonexistent government oversight (not to mention school personnel's failure to instill discipline in students, allowing them to sex, text, drink and drug away their college years). Carelessness should end.

DR. CAROLYN LADELLE BENNETT

Discipline should be instilled. Graft must be outlawed. Activity strictly monitored; and where graft is found, perpetrators should be impartially penalized. No matter who or what is involved, no matter where it is found, graft must be abolished.

Solid Workforce

Preparedness requires a strong workforce, not dependency. Private and "nonprofit" entities serving their own interests have created an addictive society. They have weakened individuals and institutions. The medical establishment does not cure; it addicts, and profits by the addiction to drugs and procedures. The same pattern is evident all across entities that declare but never realize high-sounding missions of advancement and improvement.

America must shore up its permanent workforce for current and future generations. The government regulatory apparatus is one sector that needs far more trained personnel, and it is an area that would provide solid employment. The current weakening of government can be mended and strengthened by the employment of a whole range of individuals who have been excluded from solid work and professions. The discard of young people and others to "gig" work has contributed to the weakening of the country. The mutual carelessness of employer and employee, in the gig work enterprise, results in an unhealthy society all round. As to government work, one segment of contemporary society has a penchant for disparaging "unelected bureaucrats." But their argument is a fallacious one because the America's civil service (not partisan politicians, elected officials, or appointees) is the mainstay, the buttress of government of by and for the people. Destroy the government, as wished for by wishy-washy extremists; and so too would be destroyed all possibility for a more perfect *Union*.

All solid work should not be the exclusive domain of government, but government work needs mending. The diplomatic corps is an area that needs improvement. The Department of State needs professionals, knowledgeable, skilled, respectful people of clean and clear speech; and people who will work exclusively for the public sector. No person should be hired by the US Department of State or diplomatic corps without pertinent credentials. Any person (of the ilk of an Albright, Austin, Clinton, Nuland, Pompeo, or Power) who has demonstrated unprofessional behavior or disrespect for the position or for the United States, for other nations or for the United Nations or the International Criminal Court should be barred from employment with the government of the United States, and particularly the diplomatic corps.

ASSIMILATION AND UNION

To assimilate means to embrace, absorb, incorporate; to join, become part of, take into mind and comprehend the structure into which one enters (or is invited to enter). This does not mean that a person such as an immigrant is to be shorn (raped, violently torn) of his birth culture. It does not mean the structure into which he or she enters is perfect, set in stone, unchangeable, or dead. There is a freedom in knowing the rules; and collectively, as a society, being part of an established form. The process of assimilation provides *responsible (parts not supplanting the whole)* freedom in stability which is preferable to rupturing or razing (breaching, dividing, demolishing) the whole. Nonviolent assimilation is preferable to an anachronistic (caveman) state of warfare—preferable to chaos, tribalism, anarchism, nihilism—*and assured annihilation.*

Rabid American individualism has promulgated, incessantly and insidiously, the erroneous message that discipline prevents freedom. The truth is that discipline is essential to and ensures freedom of the whole: freedom of whole domestic and global societies—*and therefore freedom of the individual.*

I believe in assimilation. I do not believe in or support violence, violation, or rape of any kind, including rabid brainwashing. The treatment of indigenous peoples by officials attached to or employed by states, religious institutions and other groups was an abuse of power. It was illegal and immoral on its face, though wielders of power then and now have twisted law and morality to legalize and justify unspeakably profane acts.

I do not subscribe to the "any means necessary" extremism. "Necessary" is subjective notion, and the "means" is likely to be unjust, illegal, and inhumane. The whole phrase evokes violence. The manner and means used by people wielding power in sectarian and state institutions in their approach to and treatment of Indigenous peoples was wrong, *on its face*. It was inhumane in all respects. Attempting to excuse brutality by using the fallacious argument that those violated (those *others*) are "evil," are without "souls" or humanity—worsens the breach. I do not excuse abusers of power or selective groups committing wrongs to serve narrow status, sectarian or economic interests. I do not excuse bullies on playgrounds or in school corridors, bullies ensconced in palaces of the Vatican and Canterbury, or bullies situated in corporate boardrooms or presidential cabinets. I believe in strict checks on power and when those checks break down, they should be restored—not by fiat, but by just, *established* law impartially applied; not by prejudice, religiosity or zealotry, but on the basis of sound moral and ethical principles.

I believe in rules and law and order applied impartially and across the board. I do not believe in anarchy and nihilism or any philosophy or creed that says *anything goes* (*mine*, "my" "freedom" counts above all). I do not subscribe to the extremist position that says if you dislike something, if you are uncomfortable with some person, place or thing—destroy it, tear it down, decimate it.

I believe in the structured invitation to assimilate; not violent means toward assimilation. I believe that assimilation is an essential ingredient of America's Union. I believe contributive to America's unity is the codification and required learning of *standard* (correctly written and spoken) English. American English should be the national and official language of the United States America. Kindergarten through twelfth graders should be required to study English and world languages (such as African and West Asian languages) taught by qualified language teachers. Reasonable proficiency in these languages should be a requirement for high school graduation.

I support the ingenuity and constructive contribution of coats and cultures of many colors. I subscribe to *no* form or manner of extremism— including the many forms of tribalism. If individuals or groups are gated or ghettoed by choice or order—the isolation or disaffection yields self-harming ignorance, jealousy and irrational fear, smoldering resentments, and imaginings of aggression.

If people are assigned to black chairs or white chairs, varieties of colored chairs in college or university (segregated graduation ceremonies, plus segregated curricula equals separate water foundations regress), if an entrenched public official on the road to the US presidency color-codes his supporters and, in office, racially divides his nominees and appointees by perceived color-caste (master-servant) malleability, such actions block the natural, essential channel to human understanding. Such actions show contempt for (and opposition to) the Union, the US Constitution, America, its people, and society.

In Union is self-confidence without the need for extreme arrogance, domination, manipulation, or denial of others. As Allegiance to Union risks no *loss of self* to the individual—so, too, US practice of multilateralism and respectful relations with world nations poses no threat the Union of the United States of America.

We the People

A more perfect Union presupposes the existence of some measure of Union: a unity of the body politic, the people en masse, all together— not a mass of separates, tribes, sectarians, rabid partisans. Not laziness but work: people working together. Union suggests a bridge, not a breach.

The expression "We the People" does not mean nor should it mean "us" against "others." It does not mean separate from or superior to; nor does it mean less than. To love one's country (and to pledge allegiance and sing its hymns) is not to hate another country. Nor is it to view another as enemy. A people who, as a body, perceive others as their enemies are under the influence of mind control that is perpetrated by people and entities who stand to gain from controlling the minds of the masses; so much so that, as sheep to slaughter, the masses will succumb to (even applaud) the cabal's profiteering from endless aggression against perpetually manufactured enemies—*the cabal's destruction of America.* Americans manipulated by a cabal of mass media, partisan propaganda and 24/7 nonsense have celebrated their ignorance of world and national history. Under the control of banner headlines and screeching virtual sphere postings shouting the flaws, failings, and frailties of other nations and peoples—Americans distracted by the clamor have accepted unacceptable American flaws and frailties; ignored fixable failures; and contributed, mindlessly, to the death of America.

It is Americans' *extremism*, however manifest (in distractedness and backwardness, anarchism and tribalism, or militarism and nihilism), that threatens the world—and America's Union.

We are an imperfect people, as are all others. Our Union is imperfect, so we aspire *to form a more perfect Union.* "I do not expect the Union to be dissolved—I do not expect the house to fall," Abraham Lincoln said, "I do expect it will cease to be divided: It will become all one thing or all the other." The sixteenth president was speaking in the early second half of the nineteenth century. "I am exceedingly anxious," Lincoln said, "that this Union, the Constitution, and the liberties of the people shall be (preserved for future generations) in accordance with the original idea for which that struggle was made."

Perhaps again we should hear and heed Abraham Lincoln. "It is for us to be dedicated to the great task remaining before us (and to) strive on

To finish the work we are in

To bind up the nation's wounds

To care for (those) who shall have borne the battle; and for (their relations)

To do all which may achieve and cherish a just and a lasting peace among ourselves—*and with all nations* (minor edits, emphasis added).

DR. CAROLYN LADELLE BENNETT

6

A Set of Remembrances

(Alphabetical order by last name)

JULIAN PAUL ASSANGE (b. July 3, 1971) was an Australian editor, publisher, founder of a multi-national media organization and associated library known as *WikiLeaks*. The organization published evidence of crimes committed by US military and political elements (material that was republished by major US press organizations). The cabal commanding the prior crimes then set in motion the machinery of punishment. On their watch, Assange has been tormented, imprisoned, and effectively tortured by US entities and "allies." Officials of the United States (three US presidencies: Barack Obama, Donald Trump, Joseph Biden) pushed for Assange's transfer to the United States for further torture and possible death. While the British judiciary went through the motions of seriously considering the US extradition demand, Julian Assange languished (as dead) in a British prison for hardened convicted criminals. Before being abducted, Assange had been effectively imprisoned in the London-based Ecuadoran Embassy. That country's head of state at the time (2012-2019) had offered Assange asylum. After the abduction, the British imprisoned Assange in their maximum-security Belmarsh prison where he has languished from April 2019 through the time of this writing.

US gerontocrats such as Baptist minister (former governor of Arkansas) Michael Dale Huckabee, US Senator Addison Mitchell McConnell III, former US congressman Newton Leroy McPherson (Gingrich), and former Alaska governor Sarah Louise Palin were reported to have labeled Assange (*erroneously*) a "terrorist," and maliciously incited extremist elements (or anyone listening) to kill him. US officials have shielded war criminals; misused instruments of law; and, *with impunity*, violated the human rights of anyone with whom they disagree. Their actions are the death knell for law and justice.

REMEMBER editor, publisher, and truth teller Julian Paul Hawkins Assange born in Townsville, Queensland, Australia, July 3, 1971.

HARRY DUNN was a young Englishman who had not yet reached his twentieth birthday when an American ran him down with her vehicle. The case was vehicular homicide. The American who killed Harry Dunn fled England and was later prosecuted in absentia. She refused to return to England to stand trial and two US presidencies shielded her, refusing extradition to England. Despite pleas by Dunn's family, US Presidents Donald Trump and Joseph Biden barred processes of law and justice.

REMEMBER a very young man cut down in his youth by an American motorist shielded from extradition by US officials. Remember Harry Dunn 2000-August 2019.

RUSH HUDSON LIMBAUGH III set a high standard (1967–2021) in an area of radio broadcasting that few if any have achieved. Excellence in broadcasting in America ended with Limbaugh.

Mark Steyn[124] who is more Birmingham, England, than New England remembered Rush Limbaugh as a commentator "who took politics seriously but not solemnly"; and brought to radio broadcasting an unmatched and unfaltering brand of "piercing philosophical clarity," "grand rollicking presentational style"— news analysis "punctuated by

---

[124] Mark Steyn, "The Indispensable Man" Rush Limbaugh, 1951-2021," Mark Steyn pages Ave atque vale, February 17, 2021 https://www.steynonline.com/11078/the-indispensable-man

musical parodies, satirical sketches" layered with cogent content, and interlaced with "optimism and good humor." *Agreed!*

As a well-prepared performer in any art or craft, Limbaugh made a tough job seem easy. He labored but did not make the audience labor to understand him. Consistently, Limbaugh brought excellent broadcasting performance, respectfulness for audience and for the English language. His diction, delivery, and voice quality were excellent—never reduced to coarseness, insult, or offhand vulgarity. I chided him once for his "Chi-Com" usage. Limbaugh *earned* inductions into the National Radio Hall of Fame and the National Association of Broadcasters Hall of Fame; and the honor of a US Presidential Medal of Freedom. I never met Limbaugh. I was not a "fan" because I'm not fan material. But I sensed a common spirit that values hard work and loves "America the Beautiful."

REMEMBER veteran radio broadcaster Rush Hudson Limbaugh III: January 12, 1951-February 17, 2021.

YINGYING ZHANG'S LIFE, like Harry Dunn's life, had barely begun. In the United States, she was ignored and unprotected by people who should have paid attention and protected her.

A criminal abducted and *disappeared* Yingying Zhang. "We cannot imagine living our lives without her" expressed the depth of the family's mourning. Their grief was inconsolable, beyond comfort, waiting for what will never come—the return of a beloved daughter. Her father was heard to say "we are waiting for you to come back."

The young 26-year-old Yingying Zhang was a native of the Jianyang District, Nanping City, Fujian Province of the People's Republic of China. She was an outstanding international scholar. Before coming to the United States, she completed undergraduate studies "with distinction" in environmental science at Zhongshan University and completed graduate studies in environmental engineering at Peking

University. Further studies took her to the Institute of Botany at the Chinese Academy of Sciences.

In April 2017, she was a visiting scholar and researcher at an American Midwestern university, the University of Illinois. She was preparing for doctoral studies scheduled to begin in the fall semester of that year. As she was running around doing off-campus errands in early June, Yingying Zhang was struck down by a reckless American's disregard for life—anyone's life, anywhere. The life of this aspiring young scientist and teacher was taken within a few weeks of her arrival in the United States.

Yingying Zhang was born December 21, 1990. She was abducted and *disappeared* on American soil; and though the gruesome nature of her slaying was published and republished, broadcast and rebroadcast— *her body has never been found*. From the start of this incident, press organizations in the United States focused almost exclusively on the assailant and musings on the gruesome nature of the crime, feeding the lust for blood of a psychologically impaired people.

No flag of the United States of America flies at half staff for Yingying Zhang. No American entity or individual begs forgiveness, knowing full well that this egregiously unconscionable, barbarous breach—rising from pervasive callousness, criminal negligence and irresponsibility in the American culture—is *unforgivable*. Yingying Zhang was a light in darkness; a young, irreplaceable light that came in peace. She came with open mind and open heart, and bridged two great countries— indeed, *two continents*.

REMEMBER a Chinese scholar who visited America, Yingying Zhang: born in Nanping, Fujian Province, December 21, 1990 – declared dead June 9, 2017.

7

Further References and Cited Material

CAUTIONARY TALES

Eisenhower, Dwight D. "Farewell Address," delivered January 17, 1961. American Rhetoric. Authenticity Certified: Text version transcribed directly from audio Audio mp3 of Address https://www. americanrhetoric.com/speeches/dwightdeisenhowerfarewell.html

Gates, Henry Louis Jr. "100 Amazing Facts about the Negro: Did Black People Own Slaves?" March 4, 2013. https://www.africanamerica.org/topic/did-black-people-own-slaves

Keller, Helen "Our Great Responsibility" Helen Keller Archive Transcription of Helen Keller's 1931 speech advocating for world peace over war.
https://www.afb.org/HelenKellerArchive?a=p&p=about&e=-------en-20--1--txt-------2-7-6-undefined-2--------------0-1

"Inbreeding among Royals: 14 Monarchs Who Experienced the Side Effects of Incest." The Science Times Medicine and Health staff reporter January 7, 2020. https://www.sciencetimes.com/articles/24610/20200107/inbreeding-among-royals-14-monarchs-who-experienced-the-side-effects-of-incest.htm

Impact of Europe's Royal Inbreeding: Part I / Part II." Medical Bag February 24, 2014 / March 27, 2014.

https://www.medicalbag.com/home/features/grey-matter/impact-of-europes-royal-inbreeding-part-i/

https://www.medicalbag.com/home/features/grey-matter/impact-of-europes-royal-inbreeding-part-ii/

Gershowitz, Adam M. "The Opioid Doctors: Is Losing Your License a Sufficient Penalty for Dealing Drugs?" Hasting Law Journal 72, 871 (2019). Rev November 6, 2021. https://papers.ssrn.com/sol3/papers.cfm?abstract_id=3566600&msclkid=25e0f573b5d011eca02bbd80d56e9597

Gershowitz, Adam M. "Punishing Pill Mill Doctors: Inconsistent Sentences in the Opioid Epidemic." UC Davis Law review. Vol 54. No. 1053. 2020 November 5, 2021. https://autopapers.ssrn.com/sol3/papers.cfm?abstract_id=3503662&msclkid=ae04dc5eb5cf11ec9f761c8a688f1f76

Adam M. Gershowitz, William and Mary Law School Associate Dean for Academic Affairs and R. Hugh and Nolie Haynes Professor of Law https://law2.wm.edu/faculty/bios/fulltime/amgershowitz.php

Robinson, Mary. "Nuclear weapons are still the greatest threat to world peace. NATO must take action now to protect humanity." The Elders. December 3, 2019. https://theelders.org/news/nuclear-weapons-are-still-greatest-threat-world-peace-nato-must-take-action-now-protect https://theelders.org/who-we-are

Gorbachev, Mikhail S. "Perestroika and New Thinking: A Retrospective" Global Affairs August 9, 2021 (previously published in Russia in Global Affairs, an article in translation of a Russian-language text by. https://globalaffairs.ru/articles/ponyat-perestrojku/ https://eng.globalaffairs.ru/articles/perestroika-and-new-thinking/

Khamenei, Sayyid Ali. "Letter to Youth in the West." November 29, 2015. transcript MEHR News 8th of Azar, https://en.mehrnews.com/

news/168797/Review-of-Ayatollah-Khamenei-s-Letter4U-to-Western-youth)

Carnelos, Marco. "The Great Game in central Asia is over - and America lost." Middle East Eye: Campaign against Sanctions and Military Intervention in Iran. August 27, 2021 http://campaigniran.com/casmii http://campaigniran.com/casmii/?q=node/14906

The tragic epilogue in Afghanistan came as no surprise to those few analysts who knew the real dynamics of the conflict but were often ignored, or ridiculed.

TRT World Turkey October 18, 2021 "Erdogan: Turkey rejects Orientalist approach towards African continent"...: https://www.trtworld.com/africa/erdogan-turkey-rejects-orientalist-approach-towards-african-continent-50838)

Staughton, John. "Orientalism: Definition, History, Explanation, Examples and Criticism." *Science ABC*. November 13, 2021, updated January 22, 2022. https://www.scienceabc.com/social-science/what-is-orientalism.html?msclkid=69722406b12111ec98d7631b42813067

Union and the United States of America

United States Congresses – Sessions 1st through 117th

"Dates of Sessions of Congress: United States Senate." https://www.senate.gov/legislative/DatesofSessions ofCongress.htm

"United States House of Representatives. https://history.house.gov/Institution/Session-Dates/Session-Dates/ https://history.house.gov/Institution/Session-Dates/All/

Years of the 1ˢᵗ through 117ᵗʰ Congresses (1789–2022): "Since the 74ᵗʰ Congress (1935–1936), the first session of a Congress convenes on January 3 of odd-numbered years and adjourns on January 3 the following odd-numbered year."

United States Congress Wealth, Ineffectiveness

Wikipedia s.v. "Source List of current members of the United States Congress by wealth." Page last edited December 23, 2021. https://en.wikipedia.org/wiki/List_of_current_members_of_the_United_States_Congress_by_wealth

Smock, Ray. "Incivility and Dysfunction in Congress is a National Crisis." History News Network Columbian College of Arts and Sciences. October 24, 2011.

https://historynewsnetwork.org/article/142484#

https://historynewsnetwork.org/mission-statement.html

United States Founders, Founding Documents, Pledge of Allegiance

The Federalist:

No. 1 October 27, 1787 "General Introduction" by Alexander Hamilton

No. 2 October 31, 1787 "Concerning Dangers from Foreign Force and Influence" by John Jay

Federalist No. 1 General Introduction for the *Independent Journal* Author: Alexander Hamilton

To the People of the State of New York; Federalist No. 2: "Concerning Dangers from Foreign Force and Influence" for the *Independent Journal.* Author: John Jay "To the People of the State of New York".

Library of Congress Research Guides Documents in American History Federalist Nos. 1–10 Union

https://guides.loc.gov/federalist-papers/text-1-10#s-lg-box-wrapper-25493272

Library of Congress Research Guides Federalist Papers: Primary Documents in American History

Full Text of the Federalist Papers

https://guides.loc.gov/federalist-papers/full-text

https://tile.loc.gov/storage-services/service/rbc/rbc0001/2014/2014jeff21562v1/2014jeff21562v1.pdf

Library of Congress Research Guides Federalist Papers: Primary Documents in American History

Wikipedia

"John Jay." https://en.wikipedia.org/wiki/John_Jay

"Alexander Hamilton." https://en.wikipedia.org/wiki/Alexander_Hamilton

"The Federalist Papers." https://en.wikipedia.org/wiki/The_Federalist_Papers

"E pluribus unum."

https://en.wikipedia.org/wiki/E_pluribus_unum

"Publius (praenomen)."

https://en.wikipedia.org/wiki/Publius_(praenomen)

"Constitutional Convention (United States)." https://en.wikipedia.org/wiki/Constitutional_Convention_(United_States)

National Archives. "The Constitution of the United States: A Transcription."

https://www.archives.gov/founding-docs/constitution-transcript

National Archives. "Declaration of Independence in Congress July 4, 1776": a transcription of the Stone Engraving of the parchment of the Declaration of Independence, document on display in the Rotunda at the National Archives Museum. https://www.archives.gov/founding-docs/declaration-transcript)

Pledge of Allegiance (United States)

Wikipedia s.v. "Pledge of Allegiance" (Bellamy versions)

https://en.wikipedia.org/wiki/Pledge_of_Allegiance

"4 US Code § 4 - Pledge of allegiance to the flag; manner of delivery." Cornell Law School Legal Information Institute. https://www.law.cornell.edu/uscode/text/4/4

Wikipedia s.v. "National Security Agency." https://en.wikipedia.org/wiki/National_Security_Agency)

United States Language

English as US national language

"English Language Unity Act" of 2019 (H.R.997) was introduced in the US House of Representatives by Congressman Steven Arnold King on February 6, 2019.

Numbers of cosponsors: 27

If passed, the bill would establish "English as the official language of the United States," and would establish "a framework for implementation and enforcement, including by testing English as part of the naturalization process."

The latest action was the March 22, 2019, referral to Subcommittee on Immigration and Citizenship.

https://www.congress.gov/bill/116th-congress/house-bill/997/all-info

The Senate companion bill "English Language Unity Act" of 2019 (S.678) was introduced Senator James Mountain Inhofe on March 6, 2019

Numbers of cosponsors: 3

If passed, the bill would have established "English as the official language of the United States;" and established "a framework for implementation and enforcement, including by testing English as part of the naturalization process."

The latest action was March 6, 2019 two readings and a referral to the Committee on Homeland Security and Governmental Affairs https://www.congress.gov/bill/116th-congress/senate-bill/678

Library of Congress. H.R.997 - English Language Unity Act of 2019 116th Congress (2019-2020) introduced by Rep. Steve King Febraury 6, 2019 (27 cosponsors) https://www.congress.gov/bill/116th-congress/house-bill/997/all-info

Library of Congress S.678 - English Language Unity Act of 2019 116th Congress (2019-2020) introduced by Sen. James M. Inhofe March 6, 2019 (3 cosponsors) https://www.congress.gov/bill/116th-congress/senate-bill/678

United States' Officials Call to End War

Library of Congress "H.R.608 – "Stop Arming Terrorists Act." 115th Congress (2017-2018). Introduced in the House by Rep. Tulsi Gabbard January 23, 2017. 14 cosponsors.

https://www.congress.gov/bill/115th-congress/house-bill/608

https://www.congress.gov/bill/115th-congress/house-bill/608/all-info?r=30&s=3

Library of Congress S.532 – "Stop Arming Terrorists Act" 115th Congress (2017-2018) introduced in Senate by Sen. Paul, Rand March 6, 2017. https://www.congress.gov/bill/115th-congress/senate-bill/532

Huff, Ethan. "Rand Paul introduces "Stop Arming Terrorists Act." Rand Paul news. March 22, 2017.

https://www.randpaul.news/2017-03-22-rand-paul-introduces-stop-arming-terrorists-act.html

Ban Killer Drones. "DANGERS: Weaponized Drones – Unprecedented power to kill and traumatize with minimal or no consequence to the perpetrator" (paper). https://bankillerdrones.org/dangers/

State of United States

Wikipedia

Union Pacific Corporation. https://en.wikipedia.org/wiki/Union_Pacific_Corporation

Union Pacific Railroad: Notable Accidents. https://en.wikipedia.org/wiki/Union_Pacific_Railroad#Notable_accidents

Hydrochloric Acid.

https://en.wikipedia.org/wiki/Hydrochloric_acid

BNSF Railway.

https://en.wikipedia.org/wiki/BNSF_Railway

THE WORLD
ASSEMBLIES, DECLARATIONS, NATIONS SOVEREIGNTY, HUMAN RIGHTS, SECURITY, LANGUAGES

Nations in Cooperation

Nations Online. "Map of the Commonwealth of Independent States" (Armenia, Azerbaijan, Belarus,

Kazakhstan, Kyrgyzstan, Moldova, Russia, Tajikistan, and Uzbekistan; associate member Turkmenistan). https://www.nationsonline.org/oneworld/map/CIS-map.htm

The Organization of American States https://www.oas.org/en/about/who_we_are.asp

The OAS dates back to the First International Conference of American States held in October 1889 through April 1890 in Washington, DC. The stated reason for establishing OAS was "to achieve among its member states ... 'an order of peace and justice, to promote their solidarity, to strengthen their collaboration and to defend their sovereignty, their territorial integrity, and their independence' (as written in Article 1 of its charter). The OAS is headquartered in Washington, DC.

Union of South American Nations https://www.unasursg.org/

The UNASUR was established 2008. It is a consensus mechanism made up of Argentina, Bolivia, Brazil, Chile, Colombia, Ecuador, Guyana, Paraguay, Peru, Surinam, Uruguay, and Venezuela that "has become the preferred scenario for political dialogue and consensus in South America." Toward strengthening bilateral relations of Colombia with the region, "this forum has fostered the creation of a new way in which the countries relate with others."

https://www.cancilleria.gov.co/en/union-south-american-nations-unasur

Wikipedia.
Union of South American Nations. https://en.wikipedia.org/wiki/
Union of South American Nations

Related links: http://www.comunidadandina.org/
sudamerica.htm

http://www.pptunasur.com/

Caribbean Community https://caricom.org/member-states-and-associate-
members/
https://caricom.org/

Among Caribbean States, CARICOM is "the oldest surviving integration movement in the developing world" that has also become "a respected voice in international affairs." CARICOM was established on July 4, 1973, with the signing of the Treaty (rev. in 2002) of Chaguaramas by Prime Ministers Errol Barrow for Barbados, Forbes Burnham for Guyana, Michael Manley for Jamaica and Eric Williams for Trinidad and Tobago. Represented in the current organization are approximately sixteen million people (60 percent of them under the age of 30): Indigenous Peoples, Africans, Indians, Europeans, Chinese, Portuguese and Javanese speaking many languages, including English (the major language) along with French and Dutch and variations of these; and African and Asian expressions.

Community of Latin American and Caribbean States https://
celacinternational.org/
https://en.wikipedia.org/wiki/Community of Latin American and
Caribbean States#Member states

CELAC was formed in 2011 in Caracas, Venezuela, with the signature of the Declaration of Caracas; and for some 650 million people comprising the region of Latin America and the Caribbean. The organization's stated purpose was "to deepen respectful dialogue among all countries in the region in areas such as social development, education, nuclear disarmament, family farming, culture, finance, energy and the environment."

Thirty-two sovereign countries speaking four different languages in the Americas make up the Community of Latin American and Caribbean States (CELAC)

United Nations

United Nations. Charter of the United Nations. https://www.un.org/en/about-us/un-charter/full-text

United Nations

> The United Nations is composed of 193 member states as of 2022.

> The United Nations Security Council is composed of five permanent: the People's Republic of China, the French Republic, the Russian Federation, the United Kingdom of Great Britain and Northern Ireland, and the United States of America.

> Calls for reform have centered on the UNSC's

- Membership
- Veto held exclusively by five (China-France-Russia-UK-USA) permanent members
- Regional representation
- Size of an enlarged UNSC (the current UNSC has ten nonpermanent members)
- Working methods
- UNSC relationship with the UN General Assembly

United Nations. https://www.un.org/en
United Nations, "About us." https://www.un.org/en/about-us

Wikipedia.
"Reform of United Nations Security Council." https://en.wikipedia.org/
wiki/Reform_of_the_United_Nations_Security_Council

"United Nations Security Council." https://en.wikipedia.org/wiki/
United_Nations_Security_Council

United Nations High Commissioner for Refugees United Nations High
Commissioner for Refugees: The UN refugee Agency "2030 Agenda
for Sustainable Development."
https://www.unhcr.org/2030-agenda-for-sustainable-development.
html?msclkid=059816afb10e11ec8a3084e2f445c178

United Nations Department of Economic and Social Affairs Sustainable
Development. https://sdgs.un.org/goals

United Nations High Commissioner for Refugees (UNHCR)
headquarters Geneva, Switzerland.

Universal Human Rights

Wikipedia.
Universal Declaration of Human Rights
https://en.wikipedia.org/wiki/Universal_Declaration_of_Human_
Rights?msclkid=62f16dd5b2a711eca5aa3d330382f39c

United Nations
https://www.un.org/en/about-us/universal-declaration-of-human-right
s?msclkid=06073dc2b2a611ec9069b1095daa914e

United Nations.
https://www.un.org/en/about-us/udhr/drafters-of-the-declaration

Youth for Human Rights.
https://www.youthforhumanrights.org/what-are-human-rights/universal-declaration-of-human-rights/introduction.html

International Relations.
https://theinternationalrelations.com/universal-declaration-of-human-rights-udhr/#:~:text=The%20document%20which%20later%20become,the%20General%20Assembly%20in%201946.?msclkid=46acbac0b2b011ec89163b1f66d895b9

Infogalactic.
Peng Chun Chang. https://infogalactic.com/info/Peng_Chun_Chang?msclkid=f64e12b2b2aa11ec9d2236b8c7718ab6
Charles Malik. https://infogalactic.com/info/Charles_Malik

Eleanor Roosevelt. https://infogalactic.com/info/Eleanor_Roosevelt

Canadian Encyclopedia, The. John Peters Humphrey. https://www.thecanadianencyclopedia.ca/en/article/john-peters-humphrey?msclkid=09eab853b2ac11ec8af73c8fe0182ee5

"Sanctions are 'US way of war'." President Seyyed Ebrahim Raisi of Iran addresses the general debate of the UN General Assembly's 76th session. UN Affairs. UNTV. September 21, 2021. https://news.un.org/en/story/2021/09/1100572

"United States Sanctions are Crimes against Humanity." Press TV June 3, 2021 https://www.presstv.com/Detail/2021/06/03/658205/Iran-United-States-sanctions-crimes-against-humanity-war-crimes-United-Nations-envoy-Takht-Ravanchi

"World must hold US to account for supporting Daesh, new terrorism: President Raeisi." [President of the Islamic Republic of Iran Sayyid Ebrahim Raisolsadati (Ebrahim Raisi)] Press TV news. September 5, 2021. https://www.presstv.ir/Detail/2021/09/05/665904/Raeisi-Macron-Iran-Afghanistan-Lebanon-US-Daesh-JCPOA-terrorism

McGovern, Ray. "Assange To Be 'Moved Around' Sine Die." July 8, 2021. https://original.antiwar.com/mcgovern/2021/07/08/assange-to-be-moved-around-sine-die/

Lauria, Joe. "The Espionage Act & Julian Assange — Part 1: A History of Prosecuting Speech." *Orinoco Tribune*. July 16, 2021. https://orinocotribune.com/the-espionage-act-julian-assange-part-1-a-history-of-prosecuting-speech/

AFL-CIO Reports. "Examining the Root Causes of the Central American Refugee Crisis." March 20, 2013. https://aflcio.org/reports/examining-root-causes-central-american-refugee-crisis www.aflcio.org

Villeda, Suyapa G. Portillo and Miguel Tinker Salas. "The Root Cause of Central American Migration Is US Imperialism." *Jacobin* Magazine. June 8, 2021. https://jacobinmag.com/2021/06/kamala-harris-central-america-guatemala-visit-us-imperialism

Granma national news staff, June 11, 2021: "Sovereignty, self-determination and independence are not on the table." http://en.granma.cu/cuba/2021-06-11/sovereignty-self-determination-and-independence-are-not-on-the-table

Leydis, Gladys and Ramos López. "We defend the Revolution, above all else." *Granma* news. July 12, 2021. http://en.granma.cu/cuba/2021-07-12/we-defend-the-revolution-above-all-else

Cyberspace, Sovereignty, Human Rights

"Russia seeks productive dialogue with US on cyber security — Lavrov." TASS news agency. June 24, 2021 https://tass.com/politics/1306651

"'Remain vigilant' against malicious technologies that could imperil future generations" UN news. June 29, 2021. https://news.un.org/en/story/2021/06/1094992

"Pegasus: Human rights-compliant laws needed to regulate spyware." UN news. July 19, 2021. https://news.un.org/en/story/2021/07/1096142

Zhihao, Zhang. "US poses 'biggest threat to global cybersecurity', ministry says." *China Daily*. July 29, 2021. https://www.chinadaily.com.cn/a/202107/29/WS61027b2ea310efa1bd66556f.html

World Languages

> *Wikipedia.*
>
> "Languages of Africa." https://en.wikipedia.org/wiki/Languages_of_Africa
>
> "Languages of the African Union." https://en.wikipedia.org/wiki/Languages_of_the_African_Union
>
> "Languages of Asia." https://en.wikipedia.org/wiki/Languages_of_Asia
>
> "List of languages by number of native speakers." https://en.wikipedia.org/wiki/List_of_languages_by_number_of_native_speakers
>
> "List of Most Commonly Learned Foreign Languages in the United States." https://en.wikipedia.org/wiki/List_of_most_commonly_learned_foreign_languages_in_the_United_States
>
> "How many languages are there in the world?" The Intrepid Guide, January 1, 2020.

https://www.theintrepidguide.com/how-many-languages-are-there-in-the-world/

Ethnologue Languages of the World.

https://www.ethnologue.com/about

InfoPlease s.v. "How many Languages are There." https://www.infoplease.com/world/social-statistics/how-many-languages-are-there

"National Language." https://en.wikipedia.org/wiki/National_language

Nations Online. "Languages of the Americas: One World - Nations Online List of official, national and spoken languages of North America, Central America, South America and the Caribbean." Sources: Ethnologue, ISO Country Names (ISO 3166-1), ISO Languages Names (ISO 639-1), CIA World Factbook and others. https://www.nationsonline.org/oneworld/american_languages.htm

PARALLEL SOCIETIES

"Government announces crackdown on 'non-Western' neighborhoods." The Local (Denmark). March 18, 2021 https://www.thelocal.dk/20210318/today-in-denmark-a-round-up-of-the-latest-news-on-thursday-5/

"Denmark removes neighborhoods from 'ghetto' list of deprived areas." The Local Denmark. December 1, 2017 https://www.thelocal.dk/20171201/denmark-ministry-removes-neighbourhoods-from-ghetto-list-of-deprived-areas/

"Fighting 'parallel societies' Danish government wants to cap number of 'non-western' residents in neighborhoods at 30%." RT news. March 18, 2021. https://www.rt.com/news/518418-denmark-non-western-residents-limited/)

Internal Displacement Monitoring Centre (IDMC). 3 Rue de Varembé, 1202 Geneva, Switzerland. https://www.internal-displacement.org/about-us

INTERNATIONAL FIGURES

Kremlin. "Vladimir Putin Biography" http://en.putin.kremlin.ru/bio/page-0

The Supreme Leader of Islamic Republic of Iran Sayyid Ali Hosseini Khamenei (Ayatullah Haajj Sayyid Ali Khamenei) biography https://www.leader.ir/en/biography

Wikipedia.

"Abigail Adams." https://en.wikipedia.org/wiki/Abigail_Adams
"John Adams." https://en.wikipedia.org/wiki/John_Adams
"John Quincy Adams." https://en.wikipedia.org/wiki/John_Quincy_Adams
"Samuel Adams." https://en.wikipedia.org/wiki/Samuel_Adams
"John Adams, Sr." https://en.wikipedia.org/wiki/John_Adams_Sr

National Archives. "Meet the Framers of the Constitution." Biographical Index of the Framers of the Constitution. https://www.archives.gov/founding-docs/founding-fathers

ACKNOWLEDGMENTS

My sincere appreciation to the Xlibris staff (manuscript representatives, copyeditors, book designers, and graphic artists). No copyright is claimed in material authored by others. I am responsible for the textual composition, compilation, and commentary contained in this work.

ABOUT THE AUTHOR

Dr. Carolyn LaDelle Bennett is a prolific Southern-born American writer and author of several books concentrating on US politics, public affairs, and international relations. Her university credentials are in education (PhD) and journalism and public affairs (MA). Bennett has worked in several US states and the District of Columbia as a university professor and as an employee with the US government. She began her career as a secondary-school teacher with the US Peace Corps assigned to Freetown, Sierra Leone (West Africa). In addition to her lifelong *labor of love* (writing), Bennett enjoys good music and capturing wildlife and cloudscapes on camera; chasing a Full Moon, winter retreats at Niagara Falls; neighborliness, civil debate, and engaging conversation anywhere. Her travel journal and camera files have recorded three continents (in North America from Campobello Island to San Francisco Bay, Lake Itasca to the Mississippi River Delta).

The short titles of her books are:
America's Human Connection (University Editions Inc)
Mary McLeod Bethune: An Annotated Bibliography (Edwin Mellen Press)
Talking Back to Today's News (PublishAmerica)
Women's Work and Words Altering World Order (Iuniverse Inc)

PUBLISHED BY XLIBRIS
Missing News and Views in Paranoid Times
Breakdown
Same Ole or Something New
No Land an Island No People Apart
Unconscionable
Pondering Alphabetic Solutions
Solutions 2
Betrayal: Public Welfare Abandoned for Private Wealth

INDEX

K

Keller, Helen Adams (Helen Keller), 14,
 161, 168–69, 177
Kennedy, John Fitzgerald, 5, 20, 85
Khamenei, Sayyid Ali Hosseini
 (Khamenei, Ayatullah Haajj
 Sayyid), 143, 177–78, 214, 218
Khamenei, Seyyed Ali (Ayatollah,
 Supreme Leader of The Islamic
 Republic of Iran), 177–78, 218
King, Steven Arnold, 114
kleptocracy, 57, 61, 93, 184
kleptocrats, xix, 8–9, 11–12, 73, 81,
 187
Kolodny, Andrew (MD), 72–73
Kremlin, 32, 44, 96–97, 147, 218

L

Language, 113–15, 118, 120–21, 124,
 131, 217
Languages of Africa, 216
Languages of Asia, 216
Languages of the African Union, 216
Languages of the Americas, 217
Languages of the world, 124, 217
Latin America, 58, 155, 211
Lauria, Joe, 215
Leah, Patrick, 5, 152, 155
Leydis, Gladys, 139, 215
liberalism, 60
liberals, xviii, 151
Library of Congress, 114, 162
Limbaugh, Russ Hudson, III, 198–99
Lincoln, Abraham, xiv–xvi, 122, 190,
 195–96
López, Ramos, 139, 215

M

Madison, James (U.S. President), ix,
 122, 190
Malik, Charles, 166, 214
Manchin, Joe, 5
Marco, Carnelos, 52
Marshall, Thurgood, 18–21
McConnell, Mitch, 5, 7, 197
McGovern, Ray, 215
media, xviii, 2, 22, 30, 63, 66, 73, 78,
 83, 115, 121, 129, 131, 135, 145
Middle East Eye, 52
militarism, 161, 195
Morrill Act, 122, 190
Mott, Lucretia Coffin, 23
multilateralism, 127, 139, 159, 194

N

Nader, Ralph, 32
National Archives, 19, 218
National Guard, 86, 106
National language, 217
National Lawyers Guild, 88
National Nuclear Security
 Administration, 37
neoliberals, xviii
nihilism, xviii, 181, 192–93
9/11 wars (War on Terror), 42–43, 94,
 152, 173
nineteenth century American women,
 169
Nixon, Richard Milhous, 49, 85
North America, 155, 178, 217, 221
North Atlantic Treaty Organization
 (NATO, OTAN), xx, 46,
 154–55, 159, 188
Nuclear weapons, 159
Nuland, Victoria, 90, 119

O

Obama, Barack Hussein, II, 10, 12, 20, 34, 85, 87, 91, 116, 119, 197
Occident, 145
official language, 113, 115, 124–26, 193
117th Congress, 5, 55, 82
One World Nations Online, 217
OpenSecrets ("Top Pharmaceuticals / Health Products donors and Top Recipients"), 68–70, 98
Organization for the Prohibition of Chemical Weapons (OPCW), 50–51
Organization of American States (OAS), 88, 210
Orient, Oriental, Orientalism, 144–45
Orinoco Tribune, 38, 40, 215
otherness, 145

P

Pakistan, 11, 17, 33, 41–42, 53, 90, 115, 120, 124, 126, 154, 167, 173, 175
Palestine, 135, 150, 153, 157
Palestinian, 151
parallel societies, 17, 20, 217
patriotism, 2, 168–69
Paul, Randal Howard (Ran), 163
Pegasus, 47, 149, 216
"Perestroika and New Thinking: A Retrospective," 160
Physicians (prescription drugs), 71, 73
Pill Mill, 74–75
Pledge of Allegiance (United States), 169–70
poverty, xx, 31, 109, 138, 150, 174
Power, Samantha, 89–90
preparedness, 9, 14, 82, 180, 182, 191

Press TV, 31–33, 38–40, 43, 46–47, 50, 52–54, 104–5, 143, 150, 153, 214
progressives, xviii
public trust, 81
"Publius," x
Purdue opioid makers, 71–72
Putin, Vladimir, 25, 116, 145, 147, 180, 218
Pyatt, Geoffrey, 119

Q

qualified teachers, 63, 189

R

Reagan, Ronald Wilson, xii, 57, 85, 91, 160
Recipients of Drug Industry contributions, 69
red lines, 44
rights, xii, xvii, 1, 43, 59, 62, 79–80, 148, 165, 177, 180
Robinson, Mary, 159
Robinson, Paul, 33, 51
Romney, Mitt, 5
Roosevelt, Anna Eleanor (Eleanor Roosevelt), 7, 24, 88, 165–66
Roosevelt, Franklin Delano, 24–25, 60, 88, 165–66
RT, 30, 32–33, 36, 38–41, 44, 46–48, 51, 94, 96–98, 102–4, 106, 132, 135, 150–54, 218
Russia, 24, 30, 32–33, 36, 39, 44, 51–52, 54, 58, 96–97, 115, 120, 126, 147–50, 155
Russian Federation, xxii, 25, 54, 116, 120, 144, 147–49, 159–60, 212
Rutgers University, 121